Make Your OWN Way

One Family's Story of Breaking the
Mold and Achieving Independence
in American Agriculture

Make Your OWN Way
ISBN: 978-0-578-68050-7 Paperback
ISBN: 978-0-578-68051-4 eBook

For permission to reprint portions of this content or bulk
purchases, contact raboufarms@gmail.com

i

DEDICATION

To my father and mother, Edward and Evelene Rabou. When you both enter the gates of heaven and meet each other again, the Lord will say, "Well done, my good and faithful servant". You have given your children the example of what a good marriage is all about. You have given your children the gift of self-confidence and the ability to stand for what is right and to do good, all while in the presence of adversity. You have blessed them with the understanding of where true joy comes from. And you have given your children your love and your support – always, without fail. I shall consider myself so fortunate and blessed if I can provide my children with the same.

To my grandfather and grandmother, Frank and Dorothy Rabou. After the passing of my father, your only son, the three years we spent together will live in my heart forever. I know your spirits were broken and could never be repaired. But I am thankful every day that we had that time together. I learned so much from you that many family members refused to see. Your undying love for and commitment to one another was an extraordinary example. The incredible struggles you faced for so many years and the sacrifices you made for others who may never appreciate or understand what you did for them is beyond reproach. Not a day goes by without my thoughts of you. And not a day will go by without my heart aching to see you again.

To my sister, Wendy Rabou Jacoby. I know this journey has not been easy for you either. But you have stuck by your brother and loved me every step of the way. You have not shed one drop of resentment or selfishness, even maybe when you were justified in doing so. Instead, you support me, you love me and you encourage me. Thank you. I love you.

To my loving wife, Julie. I love you.

And to three amazing young men who I know will make
this world a better place.
My sons, Carson, Spencer & Mason.

Because of the events written about in this book you now
have the freedom to choose your own destiny.

Other works by Ron Rabou

"Keep it Simple: The 12 Core Values that Lead to
Personal and Professional Success"

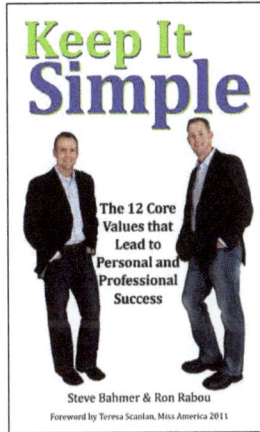

CONTENTS

FOREWORD

Agriculture has been a part of mankind since before we first walked the earth. The ground provides for us the nutrition to sustain life itself and gave to us our very own being. In the Bible, Genesis chapter 2 verse 7 states, "Then the LORD God formed a man from the dust of the ground and breathed into his nostrils the breath of life, and the man became a living being." As time progresses, technology and the reliance on man-made things has overtaken our world and we have begun to lose the connection with where we have all come from. With the hustle and bustle of life, the commitments and obligations we take on, and the need to seek attention and acceptance through sources such as social media, though the world is more connected than it has ever been, we as people are more disconnected than we have ever been.

As I sit in restaurants around our great country and observe others, I can't help but notice everyone's infatuation with their technology devices and their lack of engagement with each other, even as they sit together at the same table. We are incredibly impatient with other drivers and road rage is taking over our highways. We see no problem in flipping people the "bird" and yelling obscenities when we don't get our way. Stories, whether they are true or not, are fabricated about others so they don't get elected to political positions and it often destroys their lives. Our quest for "tolerance" of others only carries merit when we completely accept their behavior. We have become so worried about popularity and what others are doing, we fail to pay attention to the things that matter most in our lives. In fact, I think it's fair to say we fail to even know what those even are. What we have done is lost our perspective. A society engulfed in its own selfish desires is one that only serves the individuals, rather than the population in its entirety.

Many of us know we are disconnected and so to find ourselves we resort to nature. Millions of people find solace when they retreat to hike, climb, fish or just relax with Mother Nature. The outdoors are full of tremendous beauty, untouched landscapes, trees, mountains, water, flowers, wildlife and fresh, clean air. It's a place that revolves around God's Creation. No matter how sophisticated we get, how fast paced we live, and no matter how much money we make, we all have a desire to get back to our roots; to find ourselves in the natural world God created so we can reflect, relax and find peace. Most of us, if we look far enough back in our lineage, will most likely find these roots to be in agriculture. At one point in time or another, that's where we all started. That's why we have a desire to go back. To be in nature and to reconnect with the earth; and when we do, we have a renewed perspective and can refocus on our own lives and the things that are the most important to us.

We all have a story. The things that happen to us and the circumstances that surround us in our lives help to shape us into who we are. These events and circumstances help to develop unique personalities, skills, ideas and beliefs. There are people from all over the world that sacrifice all they have for the chance to come to America, and there have been thousands of lives lost in the desire to explore and develop uncharted territories within our own nation. Hundreds of years have created one of the most diverse cultures in the world. Our people are full of talent, ideas, innovation and expertise. It's exciting to see the amazing things we have done and the things that are on the horizon. However, along with this has come more divisiveness. We are divided on social issues and issues revolving around politics and religion, perhaps more so than we have ever been. Those divisions are beginning to stifle our ability as human beings to function safely, creatively and effectively with one another. Our focus has turned from harmony, peace and understanding amongst ourselves, to anger, hate and slander. Our focus has turned to power and money. Though our politicians speak of compromise and tolerance, they are shaping a system that is everything except that.

It is time we come together and realize that we are all much more alike than we are different. It is time that we focus on the things that bring us together as people, not pull us apart. It is time to focus on the things that make us great; the things that have driven our ability as Americans to help create the most prosperous nation and society the world has ever known. It is time we turn to our roots and we take that moment to reconnect during a picnic by the lake or sitting in nature listening to her quiet yet powerful presence. It is time to reflect and learn not only about who we are, but also where we come from. It is time we decide, as free people, that we do not have to be held in bondage by our heritage or our past mistakes. It is time we recognize that in the freest country the world has ever known, that we are free to choose; free to choose to become whoever we want to be, free to choose to become whatever we want to become and free to understand that the only thing standing in the way of our own success is ourselves. It is true, we all have a story. In the following pages, this is mine.

Chapter 1

IN THE
BEGINNING

My roots run deep in Wyoming, five generations to be exact. With its nearly 98,000 square miles of open space and less than 600,000 residents, Wyoming isn't exactly a mecca for crop production agriculture. Our farm is located at over 5300 feet elevation and we receive an average annual precipitation of around 16 inches. When the wind blows, as it frequently does, at 60 to 70 miles per hour, it can be an extremely lonely and frustrating place to live. There are many days where I think it would be great to live where the weather isn't so harsh, but there is something here that continues to hold me. It can be an amazingly peaceful and beautiful place too.

I've always had a lot of questions about why my ancestors moved here in the first place and what transpired over more than a hundred years to hold them here. When I've had to undergo what has seemed like, at times, insurmountable odds, I've sometimes wondered that about myself too. As I look across Wyoming's vast plains, I can't help but think "why would anyone want to live here?" I joke with people who remark about the desolation of our state that I can only imagine the folks who traveled across this land just a short time ago and what they must have thought. "Geez, this is beautiful! There are no trees, no water, the weather is horrific and there is nothing for miles on end. Let's settle down here!" I envision the emoji with the "OMG, what just happened" look with its eyes as large as saucers.

I envision that because that is how I sometimes feel. When the wind blows at hurricane force and the cold seems to never cease, it's hard to remember the days that are so nice. It's easy to lose perspective and forget about the tremendous peace that wraps itself around what we do and where we live. When I stop to think about it, I suppose no place is perfect in every respect. Afterall, the grass always appears greener on the other side of the fence.

My mother is from the East Coast and it was always amusing to me when we would visit her home state and most people there still thought we didn't have running water or motorized vehicles. You can have a lot of fun with that! Though we are not heavily populated, surprisingly enough, we do have all the modern conveniences you would expect in today's world. And yes, Starbucks is here too. The price of property here is still reasonable and no state income tax and very low property taxes make it a very tax friendly state to reside in. Thanks in large part to the Wyoming wind, the air quality is great (when the wind slows long enough to catch your breath).

The joke here is we have two seasons: winter and construction. But the truth is, our summers are mild and even when it's blazing hot in the day, the temperatures at night are nearly always cool. It's true that the winters are very long, but the fall is beautiful and helps to prepare us for what lies ahead. When night falls, it's dark. So dark, you can see every star and every constellation in the sky. When the meteor showers arrive in August, you can lie down listening to the creatures of the night and witness the folly of countless falling stars. It's truly a sight that only God could create so perfectly. Afterall, I think the folks who moved West to settle, came here in search of a better life, hoping to discover the opportunities that lie waiting for them. When they settled here, though many left, the ones who stayed were very proud to own their piece of America and to pursue the American Dream.

One of the aspects I really enjoy about living in Wyoming is that, for the most part, people are honest and trustworthy and will do what they say.

A handshake still means something here. If you get stranded on the road and swing into the nearest house, chances are the people there will be very glad to help you in any way they can. Here, you can still walk down the streets and look at passers-by in the eye and say hello. Folks around where I live still leave their houses unlocked and their keys in their vehicles. There's just no reason not to trust.

A Wyoming governor once described our state as a small town with very long roads. It's true; there's almost no place I can go in Wyoming where I don't know someone. Cheyenne, whose population is less than 60,000 is Wyoming's capital and its largest city. Only two cities in the state have a population over 50,000 and its third largest is just over 30,000.

I live near a small town in the southeastern corner of the state just 50 miles northeast of Cheyenne, population 180. Like many of you, I went to school in the same building from kindergarten through 12th grade.

My grandfather was in the first class that graduated from the same school and my father graduated from there in 1959. I joke that my high school graduating class of 12 was all girls – except for 9 guys. The dating scene was tough. Most of us dated students from other schools and to go out to dinner and a movie was a 100-mile round trip commitment.

Our class was very close and 7 of us had been together since we were in kindergarten. Our FFA chapter had won many state titles and our class was not an exception to that, having won the overall state FFA competitions when we were sophomores. In our graduating year of 1991, our class won the 9th state basketball title for our school. It was a David and Goliath story and a time in my life I'll never forget. Considering our opponent's size and talent and the fact they had won a larger division state title the year before, no one expected our small group of farm and ranch kids to win. But we did; by a very decisive 23 points.

Even today, I think there is tremendous value in living in rural America and attending a small school. Quite frankly, it's why I live where I do and why I do what I do. Afterall, if you make purposeful and thoughtful decisions, you can create a life for yourself that is exactly what you want it to be, no matter where you live or what kind of situation you find yourself in. In a nutshell, your life is what you make it. Because we live in a world that is so connected with technology and improved traveling capabilities, the geographic location of where you live no longer serves as a major constraint to what you choose to do.

The danger, however, in living in rural and small-town America, is we have more of a tendency to develop the ego of a "big fish in a small pond". The world where we live is much smaller than those who live in much higher populated areas and as a result, our perspective can be much different. Let me use myself as an example. Once I left home after high school it became quite evident to me that I was not near the caliber of athlete I thought I was. When I was growing up, I also felt our family had a big ranch, unparalleled by others. I also found out that was not true.

I grew up on an 8000-acre cattle ranch that raised about 300 mother cows and backgrounded our calves in our own feedlots. We farmed a few hundred acres of wheat for a cash crop and raised oats, corn and hay that we fed to our cattle. That may sound like a lot to many of you, but in Wyoming, that really isn't much. And it's even less when there are four families sharing it all. On our ranch, it took about 30 acres per year to run 1 cow/calf pair. If you are in the cattle business in another state, your numbers most likely involve how many cows per acre, not how many acres per cow.

As I traveled and witnessed ag operations in other states, I quickly learned many of those operations, although smaller in acres than ours, were in a much stronger financial position, had a significantly better cashflow and had a true vision and a well-balanced tolerance for risk so the future could remain promising for the next generations.

My great-great grandfather and grandmother moved to Cheyenne from Kearney, Nebraska in 1881. He was a stone mason and helped to build the Union Pacific Train Depot and the Wyoming State Capitol. Shortly after his passing, my great-great grandmother and my great-grandfather moved east to homestead acres in 1905 where our ranching operation was eventually headquartered. Soon after, my great-grandfather's siblings homesteaded neighboring acres. Eventually, as they all moved off their homesteads, my great-grandfather would become the owner of some of these lands.

In the late 1800's and early 1900's, Wyoming was still very much the "wild west". My great-grandfather spent his days caring for his growing cattle herd with a Colt Bisley 38-40 WCF pistol strapped to his side. Those who homesteaded here were very protective of their lands and would often do whatever it took to keep and grow their operations.

While digging through family archives, I found a newspaper article that read; *Two Farmers Fight When One Impounds Forty Stray Hogs: December, 27 – George Rabou and Samuel Haldeman, farmers living in the Albin district, west of Kimball, were both injured in a fight caused by Haldeman impounding at his farm a drove of forty hogs which belonged to Rabou. Haldeman was hurt in the fistic encounter and Rabou is confined to his home with gunshot wounds inflicted according to police by Haldeman after Rabou had beat him up. Rabou was shot in the leg and chest with a shotgun. Haldeman has been arrested. Rabou will recover, according to advices had from his home Sunday."*

There is no doubt the wild west was alive and well and some of the people living there were determined to make sure it lived up to its reputation.

The ranch I knew growing up was my father, my grandfather, my grandfather's sister and my grandfather's brother's two sons and their families. As you might imagine, a ranching operation of that size wasn't able to provide near enough revenue for all the partners to live comfortably. Though the partners would sometimes take a draw at the end of the year if they were profitable, the most I ever knew my father to make in a monthly wage was $600. Yet the partners were still responsible for all interior home repairs and improvements, groceries, phone, television and their personal automobile.

I am the fifth generation of our family who has been involved with the original ranching operation. When I was growing up, my father never told me I needed to one day return to our operation. My grandfather, on the other hand, was very clear that our ranch was my destiny. His life was the ranch and he expected mine to be the same.

Without much thought to doing something else with my life, I knew one day I would eventually return to our operation to carry it into future generations. While I was moving in that direction, I'm not sure the partners ever discussed the future of the operation and how things could improve or change to create additional opportunities for other family members such as myself who may join the operation someday.

My father and I had discussions about the necessity of me developing income outside of the ranching operation so they could afford to have me work there, but I know his cousins did not have a full understanding of what it would take to make a transition. When they returned to the ranch, my grandfather and my father made sure it was fair to everyone involved and that there were adequate resources to do so.

Too many times, in family business, and I believe most particularly in production agriculture, family members return to be a part of the operation without having given great thought to why they are actually doing so. Perhaps there was no guidance or purposeful planning or perhaps that was just the "easy" or simple route to take. What often results is a family trying to carry on a business that may not fit them at all or one where the partners may not be suited to be in business with each other.

The existing partners on our ranching operation, with the exception of my grandfather, were all close in age and had developed a system that worked for them. In large part, that system involved my father carrying the lion's share of the workload and delegating jobs to his partners. Though they tried to work together when making decisions it was painfully obvious whose shoulders those decisions ultimately fell on. One of my father's cousins was always quick to blame when those decisions didn't yield the results he expected. Yet when the ranch received recognition for excellence in subjects such as conservation, though my dad may have been the primary driver behind it, he always made sure everyone received the praise. He truly understood that no matter who was pointing fingers, it was critical to function as a team even though I'm sure it didn't feel like a properly functioning or balanced team to him most of the time.

Back in my FFA days, I remember overhearing someone say that "if you are green you are growing and if you are ripe, you are rotting." That saying is completely analogous to business. There is no coasting; no neutral. Especially in today's world, growth is critical to maintain progress, profitability and future stability. The problem with our operation was it had not changed and grown significantly enough to keep pace with the changing times. With the partners' aversion to risk and the unwillingness to change with a changing world, it was clear that a wreck of major proportions was eventually inevitable. Our business had literally been "rotting" for decades and it happened so slowly, no one smelled the stench. By not grasping opportunities over the years, the business was making a turn for the worse. When the turn of the century arrived, it was as if the world of production agriculture had changed so much and the inputs had become so intensive and expensive that without proper planning and preparedness, there was almost no way to survive.

I heard my father's partners say from time to time that they wished they each had their own place. I couldn't help but wonder if the ranch hadn't been in our family, what would the partners have chosen to do with their lives? Were they there because it was the easier route? Were they there because they didn't know what else to do? Were they there because they truly loved it?

In retrospection, as my mother and I have had long conversations about my dad, had his father not expected him to become a rancher, he more than likely would have been a veterinarian. That's what he truly loved. Had things been different, I also think the other partners would have found their true passions too. Instead, I believe they all returned to the operation because they felt that was their obligation, not necessarily their choice. The long-term consequences of those decisions have led to strife, entitlement and discontentment, only thickening the plot and creating an environment that would only perpetuate itself into future generations.

I thank God every day that I had parents that encouraged my sister and I to get a college education and to see the world beyond where we lived. They traveled with us and exposed us to a life that could never have been realized from our small community. I always felt like my sister had a pretty good grip on what she wanted to do in life and what type of career she wanted to pursue and she has always been very successful in doing so. She was always free to choose because the ranching partners, for whatever reasons, never wanted to include females as part of their long-term operational or ownership plans. I, on the other hand, never felt like I could pursue what I wanted because the ranch would one day intercede with whatever my plans would be. As a result, I always felt like I was just stumbling along, subconsciously waiting for the time when I would return to the ranch. It was almost as if I could never fully commit myself to anything I had a great deal of interest in. The ranch card would always trump whatever my life ambitions were.

Through a series of events that I will describe in the following chapters, I eventually came to realize in my own life that the ambitions of my ancestors did not have to also be my ambitions. I needed to find my own and shape my life based upon my own goals and desires. Because of my connection with our deep roots in cattle ranching, I always felt like it was just something I would eventually do, just like the four generations before me. Yet, there was something that burned inside of me.

Although I value my heritage tremendously, remaining strictly as a cowboy and rancher are not who I really am. It never has been. Though I wasn't sure what it would look like, my desire had always been to somehow remain in agriculture, all while pursuing my own individual interests as well. As I will explain, unforeseen circumstances in my life would cause me to evaluate what I thought I knew. They would bring me to a place of darkness and defeat, yet they would lead me to paths that would set me free and would ultimately drive me to the realization that if I was to survive, I must make my own way.

MOVING FORWARD

There's been a lot that's happened in my family and in our family business over the past one hundred and twenty years, some of which I'm sure I'll never actually know. Thanks to my grandfather, who preserved a great deal of family history, I've had the fortunate opportunity to discover, through numerous amounts of family documents, what some of the details were long ago and perhaps why things happened the way they did. It has been an eye opener for me and the more I immersed myself in some of the details, the more questions I had.

With a better understanding of the past, I derived more clarity in the sense that every generation faces challenges and change. They are just part of life. It's not common that a family business survives so long…and more importantly, it's not common that five generations later the family members would be content and happy being involved in a business created so many years ago. What's more uncommon is that family members would be effective in working together and have enough vision to change and adapt to a new world of doing business and possess the courage to make sacrifices to carry out this vision.

Many families I know, especially in agriculture, struggle with the fair transfer of assets to the next generation and the appropriate business structure to continue the viability of that farm or ranch operation. As families grow and change it's not easy to do and most times, it's not easy to even talk about. In fact, it's so difficult, many operations cease to exist or fail to succeed when a generational transfer occurs. For many operations, the failure to communicate and properly address the issues has meant the evaporation of their existence. I know this first-hand and I've been right in the middle of it.

However, the fact remains, tough choices are just that –
they are tough and because they're tough, most will never
step up to face the challenges that arise because of them. I'll
mention it again, but the failure to communicate and make
tough choices does not change that fact that these decisions
will be made. They just will no longer be in the control of the
people who could have once made them.

My intention in the following pages, whether you are
involved or have been involved in a similar family operation,
is that you discover there is hope and you are not alone.
Nearly every farm or ranch family I have worked with is
dysfunctional in some regard. Chances are, your neighbor
is feeling and going through the same thing; you just don't
know it. When the task seems overwhelming, it's important
to understand there are solutions...good solutions...for
everyone involved. Every family has a story and I hope my
story can shed some perspective on how it's okay to change.
Although it can be enormously difficult, it's quite possible
that the necessity of change can bring about opportunities
and success never before imagined.

It's important as you read, to realize that no situation
is perfect and changing that situation won't make it
perfect either. No matter what decisions you make, you
can be assured there will be challenges, heartache and
frustrations. Yet, those decisions can also bring tremendous
improvements to your quality of life and you can build a
legacy on your own terms, in your own way, that will have
a lasting positive affect for generations.

As I have walked through history in my own family, the
one thing that remains constant is change. Change is almost
always difficult, but just because it is, doesn't mean that it
won't lead to something better. I have found in my own life
that while change has been excruciating at times, it has also
brought us to a place we could have never thought possible.

When I say that life is what you make it, I really mean it. I once had a friend tell me that when faced with a challenge, whatever decision I made would be the right one. Though I didn't really understand what he meant at the time, I have learned since then that he was correct. We can't always make perfect decisions. There are a lot of variables that exist when we make decisions and circumstances often change after decisions are made. In retrospect, we may kick ourselves and wish things were different. If we had not made a specific decision, who's to say we wouldn't be wishing that we had? There is no way to predict the future and there is no way to undo the past. What we can do, however, is make the best decisions we can with the information we have at the time and continue to refine, shape and mold our lives in the pursuit of creating the life we most desire as the circumstances in our lives continue to change. The important thing to remember is to live looking forward at all times, never glancing behind wishing things were different.

Chapter 2

THE WAY
THINGS WERE

I grew up living on our main ranch compound with all the other partners and their families. Four houses were all literally within several yards of each other except for my grandparents, who lived on their own place a mile and a half away. That living arrangement is not one I would ever recommend. I always joke with folks and tell them if they ever want to know what a family ranching operation is like, just pick the relatives that hate you the most, go into business with them and move into their backyard. Living on a ranch is great but living right next to everyone who is involved can be quite difficult. It's like being in business with all your next-door neighbors in town and knowing their history and nearly everything that happens with them both inside and outside of the house. You not only work together, but you also live together and that's not always a healthy mix.

Of course, I have many happy memories. I considered my cousin who lived next door to me to be one of my best friends at the time. He and I did a lot together and I have great memories from those days. But I also remember many times growing up and being told by my aunt and my father's cousins to "get out of here", "you stay out of our way", "you kids leave this stuff alone", "us guys have real work to do". I remember my younger cousins getting spanked by their parents with belts and fly swatters. I remember fights between everyone's dogs. I remember my cousins' mothers watching soap operas and smoking cigarettes. I remember trying to be out with my dad and being yelled at by the other partners. I remember getting in trouble and having to formally go apologize to one of the partner's wives because I was running to go see my dad and unintentionally ran over her newly planted flower garden. I remember my grandfather's sister being nosy and confrontational nearly every time my sister and I stepped out of the house to do something. It's like she was constantly looking out her window waiting for the moment to pounce.

25

And I remember being very reserved and scared to ever make a mistake because of it all.

My father would always remain calm and would emphasize that we just had to all get along. He was the peacemaker and would always smooth things over to keep the environment just healthy enough to keep things operating. Ranching is a challenging business on its own, but there is no doubt that when personal, community and family dynamics are factored in, it can be enormously difficult.

The environment in the home I grew up in was very happy. We spent a lot of time laughing, talking about life and spent many hours and short getaways with my grandparents and my dad's sister's family. I was one of those kids who always considered my parents, most especially my dad, to be my best friends. We never had a lot of money, but we had each other and that was a lot. My dad always said he was rich because he had my mother, my sister and me.

My mother is from Connecticut and she is a very proper, well-mannered, soft spoken person. She and my father believed in talking about things and working things out between each other and with my sister and me. We just never argued about much. I have great memories of a snack waiting for me every day after I got off the school bus and my mom sitting and visiting with me to learn about my day. I remember the smell of fresh baked goods when I'd enter the house and I remember the times laughing together around the television or sitting down together playing board games. We traveled together and explored new places and new ideas. In our house, I remember love. I remember laughter. And I remember peace and harmony. As strange as it seems, to this day, my sister and I both agree we never heard our parents argue. If they ever did, they certainly didn't do it around us. My mother and father were the epitome of what a loving and healthy marriage and parents should be.

I remember trips to Cheyenne to church with my parents and grandparents and I remember my grandfather always insisting that he pay when we would go out to eat afterward. I remember fantastic times at my grandparents' house playing with baby kittens, mowing, gardening, playing games, baking and hunting for Easter eggs. I remember lots of laughter with my grandmother and her never-wavering love for each of us. I remember her incredible meals and her playing the piano and singing. The world I knew inside my own family was happy and loving. And it shaped me into what I believe and who I am today.

Ron & Wendy Rabou, 1977

Ed & Evelene Rabou,
December 29, 1968

CHANGE ON THE HORIZON

As my father aged and I became a teenager, I could see that he began to handle things differently. He was spending more time on his own working at my grandparents' place. And he was spending more time working on the business side of things, helping my grandfather with the loads of paperwork that come along with running a small business. He would spend hours at night working on new ideas and writing down ideas for expansion and working with landlords. He learned about veterinary science so he could spend more time working on the cattle himself, rather than hiring a veterinarian. He spent hours learning about mechanics so he could work on equipment in order to save the ranch from having to hire so much done. He singlehandedly took on those responsibilities, all while his cousins maintained the status quo, doing the jobs they had always done. And that appeared to be fine with him. There were a lot of things that needed to be done on the operation and it would undoubtedly take everyone's effort to make it work.

As my story unfolds in the coming pages, in no way do I wish to diminish my father's partners' contributions to our family operation. They and their families are all to be commended for their ability to work together and carry the ranch operation forward. It took everyone to keep things moving. But as in every business, not everyone's contribution is equal. There must be give and take. In almost every partnership arrangement I have seen, equal shares typically don't equate to equal workloads or capabilities. That's part of what makes partnerships so difficult. Our family ranch partnership was not an exception. From the outside looking in, the partners seemed to be fairly content with their arrangement.

My father was happy to take the leadership role because that is what suited him the best. But, as his son, I always felt like his contributions far outweighed the others. I always felt like there was a sense of jealousy from the others because of his abilities, well-directed mannerisms and his charisma in working with others.

When my parents were married in 1968, they rented a house from a neighbor about a mile from the ranch. When my great grandparents passed away, my grandfather's sister was the only one living in their house, which was located on the ranch compound. My grandfather suggested she move out and put up a mobile home on the property and my parents, who would be starting a family, could live in my great grandparents' home. So that's what they did.

For 30 years, my parents worked on the house, remodeling it, improving it, insulating it, removing walls and ceilings and replacing nearly everything in the house from top to bottom. I remember my father working on the house nearly the entire time I grew up. My parents hosted many parties and family events in their home and always showed gracious hospitality to visitors and family alike. There was no doubt it had become the nicest house on the ranch.

I'll never forget my father telling us about one of his partners griping about us living in this home. His cousin told him, "It must be nice to have the nicest house on the ranch", to which my father replied, "Give me the money I put into it and you can have it." Of course, that stopped his griping and the subject was never brought up again. Typically, it's interactions like these that can chip away at morale and create devastating long-term consequences for family businesses.

One of the problems with our operation was that it had only maintained itself and hadn't grown sufficiently enough to continue to adequately support the families who lived off it. While raising my sister and I in the eighties and early nineties, my father's monthly pay was minuscule. And my mother didn't work outside the home except for substitute teaching from time to time. Unlike many other operations, ours didn't pay for most of the living expenses of the partners. Even the improvements to the homes had to be paid for out of the partner's own pockets. Things like that just never made sense. The partners had to put their own personal money into the homes, yet they could never sell their homes because the ranch owned them. The dilemma all this caused not only affected the partners' current lifestyle, but it also affected their ability to retire and to pass a profitable and progressive operation on to the next generation.

Past family dynamics played a very large role in why the business was structured the way it was. My great-great grandmother and my great grandfather had built the ranch and my grandfather and his brother were next in charge of running it. The relationship between my grandfather and his brother was strained for many, many years because of his brother's addiction to alcohol. And as you might imagine, his addiction also affected the relationship with his wife and children, two of whom were my father's business partners.

My grandfather's brother died before I was born, so what I have learned about him has come mostly from people in our community and family. Fist fights and arguments were nearly a daily occurrence between he and my grandfather. When I interviewed his daughter for a book I wrote about our family history, she described to me that living with him was horrible. He would awaken his children in the morning with a cattle hot-shot (electric shocking device) and she said his addiction and abuse became so significant that one of her brothers moved home to the ranch because he was afraid his father was going to kill their mother. At one point, just days before his death, he and his sister got in a fist fight and after he had gotten knocked down, his sister began to stab him with a pitchfork. His daughter told me she thought his sister was going to kill him.

After the death of his brother, my grandfather seemed to cling even tighter to tradition and the "way things were". Over the years, he had become so hardened and resistant to change that being around him was more than most anyone on the ranch could stand. It was very clear that until my grandfather was no longer involved, the operation would not be able to grow or change. There was just too much fear on his part about losing what had taken so long to build. My grandfather was very protective about holding on to what they had, many times to a fault.

Unfortunately, our business model had become "just don't spend anything and we'll be fine". Certainly not a good business plan as we moved into the future. Because everyone was equal partners according to the ranch Operating Agreement, all the partners shared in decision making. There was no hierarchy of command, no vision for growth, no management structure, no requirements for employment, no written job descriptions and duties, and the only plan for succession was only sons could become partners. Any son of a partner could become involved, whether they were qualified or not. There were literally no other qualitative or quantitative measures for successful transition. The sum of all these parts added up to a very poor business model.

My father had always wanted more cows, more cropping opportunities and more cropland. But those plans would have to wait for another day. His partners had expressed their desire to one day retire and I can't blame them. At the time, I think they were maybe unsure about whether any of their family members would return and I think they were looking forward to one day not having to be so involved in the day to day busyness.

As I grew older and while I was attending college, the discussions my father and I had about the ranch became more involved and more visionary about what could be done to make things work for everyone. Because of limited resources, we had determined it would be best for me to get an outside job and establish a life outside the ranch. My father would then begin to groom me to become a partner and eventually take over management of the entire operation. He was most enthusiastic about this approach because I think it helped bring him clarity about the burden of how things might unfold in the future.

My father and I were always incredibly close and we talked about everything. One thing he always told me was that I never had to feel any obligation to be involved with the ranch. He always encouraged me to go my own way. But in his heart, I knew he would love it if one day we could develop a plan where we could work together. And that's what I wanted too. There is no other person I would have rather worked with than my father. The thought of raising my children around him was exciting and I could already see how he would encourage them and spend time with them and teach them about the farming and ranching lifestyle. I could see them riding with him in the truck, feeding cows and spending time in the tractor singing songs and handing him wrenches while fixing equipment, all while wearing a shirt that said, "Grandpa's Little Helper". And as I raised my family and matured as an adult, he would be there to help guide me and encourage me too, just as he always had. That was my dream.

But on November 4th, 1999, when I returned home from my job for a couple days to help him wean calves, I found myself at the age of 26 performing CPR on my father. The dreams we had of working together, the plans we had made and the hopes we had for the future would be shattered forever. The life that I once knew would only be a memory. Nothing would ever be the same.

Frank, Ed and Ron Rabou, 1978

Chapter 3

TUMULTUOUS TIMES

My father's untimely death at the age of 58 was a devastating blow to my family. It destroyed the dreams we had. It destroyed some of the relationships we once had. And it destroyed my hope in the future. It sent me to a place I never imagined possible. It created heartache and misery like I never knew. I remember what it was like after his funeral; the emptiness; the loneliness; the sorrow. It seemed as if everyone else's life went back to normal. Everyone's except mine and my mother's and my sister's. Ours was forever changed.

As you might imagine, his death changed more than just the life of my family. It changed nearly everything. As I write this, my father's sister has not spoken to me for over 16 years. Not for what happened, but what she thinks happened. And I am the one to blame, I guess. She is not unlike some other family members and some members of our small community. They are full of jealousy and disdain and perceive to know what all has transpired since my father's passing. I learned many years ago that people will believe what they want to believe, even if it isn't true. And sometimes, most especially if it isn't true. For many years, my wife and I have stood on an island on our own. And it has provided us with a perspective and a life that we could have never gained had we not been subjected to the experiences of the past 20 years of our lives.

My father died just a week before I was planning to ask my wife to marry me. Just a few short months after we were married, we awoke to the radio alarm clock in our bedroom while the local news reported that my only male cousin with the Rabou name, who I had grown up with at the ranch, was arrested by Federal ATF agents for building pipe bombs. His father's comment to us in the following weeks was that "he would never have built those for those guys if he had known they were ATF agents!" OMG. For real, I just kept thinking he didn't just say that. I literally could not believe the world I found myself living in. One day my life is normal

37

and things are clicking along just fine and the next, I have been unknowingly launched into the abyss and find myself playing cards with a troop of monkeys who still think the world is flat.

In the following pages, the best way I can describe these past 20 years is to share with you the following letter I sent to my father's sister's son. He is the only first cousin I have on my father's side of the family and we had not communicated for over 15 years because of what he had been told by his mother, my father's only sister. When I decided I would try to connect with him on Facebook, he told me it had taken him many years to forgive me for what I had done to his mother. Up until that time I knew she was angry with me but I never knew exactly why. As it turns out, the person she was really angry with was her father. After he died, I was the only one left to blame.

As you will discover as the story unfolds, the truth has a unique way of surfacing when the time is right; and it was finally time it was known. I wrote the following correspondence in response to his comments because I was literally finished ignoring the lies and rumors that spread for so many years. As I wrote, I spoke firmly with heartfelt passion and found the burden of years of circumstances and strife begin to lift. Ultimately, this letter served as the catalyst that brought us together over a year later as we began to rebuild our relationship and the years we lost between. For that, I am most grateful. I love him like a brother.

Once again, my purpose in sharing this letter and any other correspondence is not to put anyone in a negative light, but rather to exude to you, the reader, the real emotion that exists when things change and when we find ourselves in a place we never imagined. Family matters involving money, assets and business can be extremely painful and relationships can be damaged forever.

My goal is to keep this book as real as possible so that you might understand it's okay to hurt. It's okay to be angry. It's okay to think that things aren't fair. It's okay to wish things were different. I've been there too. Too many times in business transactions, the people get lost. And when the people are taken out of the equation, everything just becomes black and white. But in the end, what really matters are the people; the relationships; the love we need and must show for each other. Business is business and change is hard, but families don't have to be destroyed because of it. And when relationships go south, never give up hope that one day they can be restored.

Most editors would tell me this letter doesn't flow appropriately. However, I find it important to share it exactly as it was written. There is a human element here that will be lost if it is changed. My feelings and emotions in this letter are just that; they are mine and the content herein is personal and real.

In an effort to protect those I am referring to I have replaced some actual names with fictitious ones.

A LETTER OF HEALING

"Dear Dustin,

I've wanted to visit with you for many years and after our correspondence via Facebook Messenger a while back, I thought it best to write you a letter because what I need to say is more important than doing it over the Internet. Your response on Messenger referencing that you thought I somehow treated your mother wrongly really didn't come as a surprise to me. I have never understood why we couldn't have all just sat down at some point and communicated about what was really happening with Grandma and Grandpa and the ranch. I have known that your mother was angry with me for some reason, of which after 16 years I still don't know why. I tried to visit with her several times about what was going on, but she refused to have a conversation with me. I finally determined that I had fulfilled what was asked of me by my father and Grandma and Grandpa and made the choice to move forward with my life in spite of the fact that the families at the ranch and your family seemed to want to have nothing to do with me. Although I didn't feel any need whatsoever to be accepted by these family members, I have always hoped that we could all at least treat each other with respect and love.

During these turbulent times, Julie and I chose to develop our own independence and have been blessed to thrive in that environment. Sixteen years brings a lot of perspective and it helps to clear the mind by allowing us to look at circumstances and events more objectively. Truth surfaces, emotions are more tempered and time helps to build character and understanding in us all. So perhaps now is the time.

I believe it is very important for you to know and understand the truth behind the events and circumstances that have transpired since my father passed away over 19 years ago. There was a very poisonous perspective that was developed by both family and community members outside of this truth. And that perspective was also developed by those who were directly involved because of clouded emotions, various levels of entitlement and unreasonable thinking. As in most cases involving family and business, the facts that surround them become lost in the frantic grab for power and money. I assure you that our family is no different. And as disappointing as it was to me initially, it helped to fuel my desire to do better and to become more. And it helped to lift me to heights that I had either left far behind or never even thought possible.

When you live in a small community or are part of a family farming and ranching operation and you step outside of the norm, people don't like it. And that makes life and some decisions really tough. I tell my kids about the story of the crabs in the bucket. If you put a bunch of crabs in a bucket, they can crawl out. Afterall, they just need to reach the top edge with a claw and pull themselves out. But the interesting part is they will never get out. And the reason they will never get out is because the other crabs in the bucket will grab them and pull them down. They'll soon stop trying and will eventually die if you leave them in there long enough. Life is no different. Everyone has lots of opinions about what you're doing, why it won't work, how they can do it better, how you should listen to them, how you don't have what it takes or how you owe them something because you're younger or less experienced. We've all heard it before. I learned the hard way a long time ago that if you listen to others instead of following your heart and what you know is right, you'll never accomplish much. You'll never realize your God-given full potential. You'll never get out of the bucket.

I have taken the time to write this letter to you because I care. I care that you know the truth and I care that we can someday once again have a normal relationship. And that includes both your mother and father. Through this heartfelt correspondence to you, I will present the facts as they are and have always been. They are undisputable and undeniable. For some reason, I was the one chosen to have to directly face the events that transpired following my father's untimely passing. I was the one who had to face the reality of the situation head on. The events I will describe to you in detail changed my life forever. Most of them I did not seek. Most, especially the events with Grandma and Grandpa, were thrown at me and I was left to sort them out. And when I did, the judgment that came from others was harsh. I have had to find peace in the fact that I do not have to justify who I am or what I do to anyone on this earth and I am ultimately held accountable only by God.

There is no doubt that I am far from perfect, but my conscience does not allow me to be comfortable with "trying to get away with things". It never has. It only allows me peace when I try to do what is right and what is good. In the events involving grandma and grandpa, my father and the ranch, all I really wanted to do was help. I wanted to do what was right and I was happy to do whatever was needed. But in return, all I really wanted to hear was "thanks". Thanks for shouldering the load. Thanks for taking such great care of grandma and grandpa. Thanks for holding it together so the rest of us could move on. But those words have never come. And they may never. But it really doesn't matter now. Those moments with Grandma and Grandpa in the years after dad's death were a true blessing and an absolute gift. The conversations we had and the moments we shared can never be replaced and they will live in my memory forever. And as hard as those years were in so many ways, I would not change them for anything.

As you know, November 4, 1999, was a day I will never forget. It was a day that changed my life forever. On this cold and windy day, I had returned home at the request of my father to help wean calves for a couple days. I don't know if you were ever around when cattle were being worked, but those days were most always extremely stressful. In the later years, Grandpa stayed away because the cattle made him too sick. Joe was usually quite agreeable, but Jim was normally moody and difficult to get along with. This day in November was no different. Jim would stand back and yell at the three of us, telling us how to do our jobs and what we were doing wrong, but of course, was never willing to step up to the plate and do it himself, or even pitch in to help. This was standard practice for him in daily ranch operations as well and though my dad would usually just brush it off, this behavior was beginning to wear him out.

While we were working cattle, Jim sorted off from the round corral and sent the cattle to Joe, who then loaded them in the tub and pushed them down the alley to Dad and I, where we would do all the vaccinations, pour-ons, etc., then kick them out to the corral. In one group, the calves jumped on each other, pushing one upside down on its back. Knowing we had only a few seconds before the calf would suffocate, Dad and I jumped to the other side of the alley, widened it and let the other calves through, but by this time the calf was dead. It was no one's fault. It just happens sometimes when working cattle.

Immediately hearing what had happened, Jim yells at the top of his lungs, from a distance of course, at my dad. His words ring in my head like it just happened today. "Goddammit Eddie!! I could have told you that was going to happen, but you'll never listen to me!" I could see the frustration in my father's eyes. This was nothing new. It happened quite frequently and though the four partners could get along for the most part, they were all very different people. As with most partnerships, someone had to manage the overall operation. Someone had to be the visionary. That someone had always been my father. But taking on this role was stressful, especially when it was clear that not everyone's contribution to the operation was equal. And incidents like this became more frequent the older everyone got.

As time passed, so did the pressures from running a small ranch. My father bore the burden of how to change things fast enough to keep up with changing times. It seemed Joe and Jim were content to just work and maintain the status quo. I am not criticizing that, but my point is that things would have to change significantly if the ranch was to continue to operate successfully into future generations. It would require everyone to fully get on board to not only accept this reality, but to be proactive in facing this challenge head on.

Dad found himself in the role of businessman along with Grandpa, sharing equally in cattle duties with Joe and Jim, sharing farming duties with Joe and Grandpa, acting as the only mechanic and the only one who would doctor cattle when it required more than vaccinations, sharing equally in ranch repairs with the others, sharing in business responsibilities with Grandpa and doing most all of the external work with insurance agents, government, landlords, etc. And when he took time off, which was rare, things ceased to operate with the precision and productivity that they did when he was around.

I do not wish to diminish Joe's and Jim's contributions to the ranch. They certainly both had their admirable qualities, worked hard, and deeply valued the ranching lifestyle. In fact, the two of them and I have had great conversations since dad's passing. And I shared some fun hunting trips with Joe during that time as well. What I am trying to explain is that things appear differently when they are observed from the outside. The three of them functioned exceptionally well together. But when Dad passed away it became very clear there were stark differences between them all. There were unspoken expectations, pent up feelings, varying degrees of jealousy and differing opinions about how things should operate. And much of this went without discussion or solutions. Without an existing framework, there was chaos.

When I was in my mid-twenties, I came back and worked for the ranch for about a year. During this time, I witnessed firsthand what happened when Dad wasn't around. In his presence, it was quite apparent that things operated more smoothly and everyone got along better. The others really looked up to him and really leaned on him for direction. But when he was absent, things were much different. One day when Dad was gone, I distinctly remember I was feeding cows with Joe and Jim. The two of them had been biting at each other a bit and when Jim smarted off to his brother, the argument would be solved with a fight. Joe chased his brother through the corral and would surely have whooped him had Jim not jumped in a tractor and driven off.

Getting back to this 4th day of November in 1999. While dad and I walked to the barn to get a rope to drag the dead calf out of the alley, I put my arm around him and asked, "Why is it that you are always the one to blame when things go wrong around here?" The other side of that is Dad was always happy to give everyone else credit when things went right. He shook his head and we returned to remove the calf by ourselves.

Two hours later, I turned to fill a vaccine gun and when I faced the alley again, Dad was lying lifeless on the ground. I jumped into the alley and put my hand behind his head. It looked like he was trying to open his mouth to say something. I told him it would be okay and just as I did, his head and neck went limp and his lips turned blue. I screamed to Joe that he wasn't breathing and we dragged dad out of the alley and started CPR.

Everything seemed completely surreal. Like I was in a dream and this couldn't possibly be happening. Our efforts seemed useless. I just kept thinking he was going to wake up and everything would be okay. We tried everything and I frantically gave him chest compressions while Joe tried to breathe life back into my father. We never stopped until the ambulance arrived and while the paramedics worked on him, I kept asking him to wake up. I begged for him to wake up. I demanded that God make him well. As I rode in the ambulance with him, I just kept expecting him to wake up. But it was too late. He was lifeless.

That night in the hospital was the longest night in my life. Knowing the reality of the situation, it seemed impossible that this was happening. You can't possibly know how this feels until you are the one experiencing it. It is frightening and life changing. And it is a moment that lives with you every day. It never leaves. Some nights it haunts you when you wake up in a cold sweat thinking there must have been something else you could have done. Or waking up sobbing because you realize that moment you just spent with your dad was only in your dreams. You can't call him, you can't write him, you can't go hunting or to the game with him. You can't talk with him about the problems and joys you have in your life and ask his advice. He will never meet your children and he will never laugh with them. They will never spend a day at grandpa's house or ride in grandpa's truck. It is an empty feeling. A feeling that lives in nearly every moment of your life.

When morning arrived the next day, the doctors concluded Dad was probably gone before he hit the ground. We gathered as family and decided to pull him off life support. I remember entering his room to spend time alone with him one last time. I remember talking with him and holding his hand, recalling so many memories we shared in this life together and telling him I loved him just one last time. I remember standing around his bed, holding hands with family and praying. And crying. And shaking. The feelings of disbelief and sorrow filled the room as we slowly watched his heartbeats disappear from the monitor. He was gone; forever.

Still in disbelief and not knowing what the future had in store I feared what the next steps in my life would be. How could I move forward? Just seven short years earlier, my best friend Justin was killed in a car accident and it affected me profoundly. No one that close to me had ever passed away. I remember telling my dad that he was all I had left. I had many friends, but those two were the most important to me. They were the ones I leaned on for everything. And now dad was gone too. How could this be? This is not what I had planned for my life. This wasn't how it was supposed to turn out. Losing him so early was completely unnatural and disrupted every part of my life to the very core.

From that moment forward, nothing in my life has ever been the same. It was the moment when things changed for me forever.

Grandpa was passionate about the ranch and loved being a farmer and rancher. He spent his entire life working diligently to help make things better for the next generation. Despite his occasional rough demeanor, he cared deeply about what he had worked for and he loved his children and grandchildren more than any of us knew. His prudent business management skills, along with the fact that he just never spent any money, were largely responsible for the success and longevity of the ranching enterprise. Of course, he wasn't perfect, and I think the other three on the ranch got tired of him griping about spending money. He was tight, for sure. One time after Dad died, Grandma's microwave caught on fire and he wouldn't spend the money to get her a new one. He thought I should be able to go to the shop, grab some parts and fix it. I tried to get him to understand that I couldn't just fix the microwave that was completely fried and melted on the inside. Grandma understood the reality of the situation, so she gave me the money out of her social security stash to buy a new microwave and I put it in for her. He was not about to spend any money on a new microwave. That was just who he was. His life experiences helped to shape him that way.

There was no doubt the ranch was a top priority for Grandpa, perhaps too much of a priority at times. And had any of us experienced what he did over the years he lived we may have very well felt the same way. Something I think we all overlooked was that he had a big heart. He truly wanted to do what was right for everyone. And he never had a desire to cheat anyone. After Johnny [my grandfather's brother] died in the sixties, Grandpa went out of his way to help Johnny's sons become part of the ranch. He made sure that they could carry on in their father's footsteps by becoming equal partners in the ranching operation. After the ranch partnership was formed with the four of them and time passed, though it wasn't perfect, they found ways to make it all work. Generations before them built what they maintained and grew over time.

There's a long history of how the ranch was built. George [my great grandfather] obviously had a strong desire to ranch and his tenacity proved successful many years after he established his original homestead west of the current ranch headquarters. Margaret Rabou, George's mother, was the one that originally homesteaded the half section where the ranch headquarters are still located. George, Johnny and Grandpa worked very diligently to pay off debts and were reasonably successful in running the ranching operation. In Johnny's later years, Grandpa is the one who bore much of the burden for keeping things together. Johnny spent most of his time drinking and argued with Grandpa almost constantly, much of that time picking fist fights with Grandpa when they were together. These became so frequent that their mother, Mabel, would try to break up the fights by hitting them with a broom. Because of it all, Joe and his wife left the ranch and moved to Montana and had it not been for Johnny's death, they may never have returned and my father would have left the ranch too. He expressed to us more than once that those days nearly drove him away from the operation for good.

Over time, George purchased his own land, land from his siblings and from his mother's estate, and as a result, the ranch had grown to slightly over 6000 acres. Grandpa and Johnny added some more land, then my father's generation added a little bit more. By the time I was in school, the ranch consisted of a little over 8000 deeded acres and ran about 300 mother cows. But in later years, though it may have looked different from the outside, there was never enough money to go around so all the partners could live comfortably. They were all very risk averse and so the ranch never grew to the size it needed to adequately support all the families who lived there. When I was growing up, the most my father or his partners ever made working there was $600/month. As the pressures from ag production continued to mount, Grandpa stopped taking a wage in the late 1980s and he and Grandma lived off their social security. He knew this would allow the other partners to raise their families and hopefully begin to build for retirement.

One thing the partners could agree on was that preservation of the ranch was a priority. When we were in elementary school, you probably remember when Jim and his wife divorced and she left with their daughter. What you may not know is that Jim's wife tried everything possible to take as much of the ranch as she could. Though it was not perfect, had it not been for astute estate planning by the partners, she may have destroyed it for good. It is one thing to have irreconcilable differences and divorce because of them. But it is a whole different thing to divorce and try to destroy someone by taking everything you can from them. That is something I will never understand. After Jim's divorce, he lived extremely lean for many years to rebuild what was lost. I am quite sure it was not easy for him.

Shortly after the divorce was over, the partners restructured and developed a plan to further protect the ranch and allow for future families to carry it forward. It was apparently important enough to all of them that the ranch stay in the Rabou name, the estate planning documents were drawn up to describe that the ranch could specifically only be "transferred to sons". In order to protect itself from women who could potentially marry men who saw an opportunity to own a ranch, or perhaps in order to keep the opportunity available to only a few, the partners must have felt justified in making this decision. Because of this language, at this point the only sons who could even inherit a share of the ranch were my father, myself and my cousin [Joe's son]. I was in elementary school when this happened and certainly had no say in or even an awareness of the negotiations of how this operating agreement was drawn up.

In addition to this agreement, the partners all agreed on a minimum value for the ranch and split it into four equal parts. Each part was the "capital account" of each partner. The values declared were low enough so a reasonable succession plan could be put in place and provide for retirement for each partner or for a death benefit to a spouse. Each partner, except Grandpa, then purchased a whole life insurance policy that was large enough to accomplish two things: 1) provide money to allow a son to purchase the capital account, allowing him entry into ownership of the company; and 2) provide enough money to enable the living spouse to continue to live without having to rely on outside income as long as they stayed living on the ranch. As part of the agreement, the spouses could continue to live in their house on the ranch, provided they didn't remarry. And it is important to note that we are not talking millions of dollars. We are talking just a few hundred thousand dollars to accomplish both requirements minimally, yet adequately. That's not much in the scheme of today's world. Just ask the ladies who have had to live lean since their husband's deaths. The amount for the widows would only be enough over time if they also received other inheritance and social security benefits.

As I was growing up, I took an interest in the ranch and spent countless hours working there. I spent nights, weekends and every summer working for no pay. I never expected it. As far as I was concerned it was just what you did when you grew up on a ranch. I didn't know anything different. When I was in Junior High, Grandpa approached me and told me he wanted me to have his share of the ranch. By the time I was in high school, he had it drawn up that I would inherit his share of the ranch upon his passing. In return, he asked in the meantime that I would be around to help when they needed it. When he was gone, I would inherit ½ of his share immediately and after working there for 5 years full-time, would inherit the other half. This was a viable option and fit within the parameters of the operating agreement. Grandpa's share would pass through his son, on down to me, still abiding by the "sons only" provision. Otherwise, had I not shown an interest, the other option is my father would have inherited Grandpa's share and he would have owned 50 percent of the operation. My father was not interested in majority ownership though. He was interested in involving me and helping our family's ranching legacy to continue.

I want to be very clear here. I never asked Grandpa to become a partner in Rabou Ranch. But in Grandpa's eyes and probably my father's, it was the natural progression of things. I would one day run the operation with my father, just as my father had done with his. My dad never pushed me to become a rancher or to even be involved in agriculture at all. He encouraged me to explore other opportunities and always supported me.

I moved forward with my life, working off the ranch, trying to come up with supplemental ways to create income so one day when the time was right, I could return to the ranch and still afford to raise a family. This was the only portion of Grandpa's estate plan that I knew anything about. Dad and Grandpa had spent a lot of time making sure that all necessary documents were drawn up and that everything was spelled out very clearly for the ranch ownership transition. And it was. But there was one fault in this plan that no one would have ever seen. If Dad were to pass away first, no one could inherit Grandpa's share, because he would have no son to pass it to or through. If this were to ever happen, Grandpa's share, because of the terms of the operating agreement, would have to be absorbed by all the existing partners. In essence, Joe's and Jim's side of the family would go from 50 percent ownership to over 66 percent overnight.

According to my father's Trust, I was to inherit his shares of the ranch. In that regard, everything worked like it should. The life insurance kicked in, I was able to purchase his shares and my mother was able to keep the balance. But the event no one saw coming was my father's premature death and it put a damper on Grandpa's estate plan. The ranch attorney informed us that Grandpa could no longer give his share to me because he no longer had a son to pass it through. Dad had passed away out of order. The fate of Grandpa's share was sealed the moment Dad took his last breath. Upon Grandpa's death, his share would be absorbed by the remaining partners of the ranch; myself, Joe and Jim. Each side of the family since George's death had owned 50 percent of the operation and that was about to change. Because of Dad's premature death, our family's side of the operation would eventually go from fifty to 33 percent and theirs would go from fifty to 66 percent. Quite frankly, that was completely unacceptable to me. Had the roles been reversed, my father would have seen the mistake in the plan and found a way for Joe and Jim to protect the integrity of their shares for their families.

After Dad's passing, the ranch partners, including myself, all negotiated and finally came to an agreement. It became clear that Joe and Jim were increasingly uncomfortable with the "sons only" provision and wanted to give their shares to their daughters. Nothing could be changed without three of us agreeing because, at this point, each side of the family still owned 50 percent. We agreed to their request and they allowed Grandpa to continue with his estate plan and pass his share to me. But there was one stipulation to that agreement. As long as the ranch stayed intact, I would own 50 percent of the capital accounts after Grandpa's passing. The compromise was that if the ranch ever sold or split, Joe and Jim would each receive 30 percent instead of 25 percent and my ownership would be reduced from fifty to 40 percent. Though I felt it was unfair that their side of the family would benefit substantially from Dad's death, I didn't feel like I had any other choice at the time, except to accept the compromise and move on. Please notice that through all of this, never did I take anything from your mother, nor did I choose at any point in time, to change anything that Grandpa had set forth years and years earlier. My desire was and has always been, to preserve what should rightfully remain on our side of the family.

Through these courses of events, this was also the time I learned I was the trustee of Grandpa's trust. Grandpa had appointed Dad the trustee of this trust at some point in time and they had chosen me as the next trustee if something were to happen to Dad. Up until the time when my dad died, I had no idea that I was to be involved in any way whatsoever. I'm sure that neither of them ever thought a back-up trustee was probably even that necessary.

I knew nothing about trusts, estate planning, running a business or being in a partnership, so I had to learn quickly. What I learned is that a trust is used primarily to protect the spouse and children of the deceased. It protects against estate taxes and probate and allows the family to keep more. Grandpa put everything he owned in his trust. That included his personal automobiles, his investments (which were primarily CDs), his share of the ranch and his personal belongings. The role of the trustee is to execute the fiduciary duties, requests and demands of the trust set forth originally by the trust maker. In other words, the responsibility of the trustee is to ensure the funds in the trust are being used for the benefit of whatever the deceased had planned them to be used for. The trustee does not receive more from the trust because of service in this capacity, nor does the trustee have any control over how the funds in the trust are to be used. It is more work for the trustee than any of the trust beneficiaries and it carries with it a great deal of responsibility.

Most of the time, and certainly in Grandpa's case, assets in the trust are to be used for the health and benefit of the surviving spouse and any small children. Grandpa's Will specified, as I discussed earlier, that his portion of the ranch was to go to me upon his death. That had not changed for well over a decade. It stipulated that the remaining assets in his trust were to be used for the exclusive use of taking care of whatever needs Grandma had. It also stipulated that whatever funds were leftover after Grandma passed, were to be split "50 percent to [my father's sister], per stirpes and 50 percent to Edward Rabou, per stirpes". This is a very important clause because what Grandma and Grandpa were saying through this language was they wanted 50 percent of their assets to go to their son and 50 percent to their daughter AND they wanted it to stay that way regardless of what happened. "Per Stirpes" means that if the beneficiary dies or is incapacitated, those funds cannot go to the spouse, but rather funnel directly to the children. If the children are not living, then it would go to their children, etc., but the important point is that it can never go to anyone outside of direct lineage. When my dad died, his 50 percent went directly to my sister and me. Conversely, had something happened to your mother before Grandpa and Grandma died, you would have been the sole beneficiary of her 50 percent.

There are two things working here: 1) Grandpa's share of the ranch, which was under the constraints of working within the parameters of the Ranch Operating Agreement when he was developing a succession plan; and 2) Grandma's and Grandpa's personal assets, which were divided equally among their two children. At the time, long before my dad died, I'm sure it made a tremendous amount of sense to pass the ranch shares to a family member who would carry on the tradition of production agriculture into future generations, even if the ranch hadn't had a specific clause for succession. If you knew Grandpa well, you know that was extremely important to him. And I'm also sure it made sense to Grandpa and Grandma that their two children would share equally in their assets so they could either add to their retirement (or in my father's case, that would have been his entire retirement), or help their children or whatever they desired. Dad had invested nearly his entire life working on the ranch, so even if I had not had an interest in the ranching operation, Grandpa would have passed his share to my father.

It was my job as trustee after Grandpa passed away to make sure that Grandma had enough money to live on and care for her health and well-being. When we all went out to eat after Grandpa's funeral, I wanted to make sure your mother knew that whatever we needed to do to take care of Grandma there were adequate resources to do so. I had assumed all along that your mother knew how Grandpa had things set up, but I wanted to clarify with her that Grandpa had appointed me trustee and that I was willing to do whatever I needed to help her take care of Grandma. Julie [my wife] told me later that she saw the look on your mother's face during this conversation. We have both suspected since then that what I told your mother must have been a complete surprise. I had no idea she and her parents had not spoken about their estate plan. I suspect your mother has extremely hard feelings toward me regarding this, but I honestly don't see how she can rightfully blame me. As far as I am concerned, she should be incredibly grateful I spent the time I did taking care of her parents and for being respectful and responsible in carrying out their wishes.

It is painfully obvious that I'm somehow the bad guy because I followed through with the commitments I never asked to be part of in the first place. What's ironic is nothing changed for her when my father passed away. In fact, nothing had changed for her in Grandma's and Grandpa's estate plan for decades. But despite this reality, your mother must have had significantly different expectations. Clear communication with her parent's years earlier could have prevented much of the anguish she has felt. From the day of Grandpa's funeral, your mother completely removed herself from having a meaningful conversation or relationship with me, my mother and my sister. All the years we all spent together and the memories we created seem now to be from a completely different lifetime.

Let's back up a couple years before I continue from this point. Since the day my dad passed away, not one person on the Rabou side of the family has so much as even asked, ever, how myself, my sister or my mother are doing. People poured in from all over the state and I still get compliments from others about my dad to this day when I travel. But never once has a Rabou family member even inquired. Quite frankly, that has told me about all I need to know. I found out from neighbors years later that when they offered to come help on the ranch right after dad died so Joe and Jim could come up and be with family, the response they received from Jim was he had a ranch to run and our family would just have to "figure it out". Not the response I would expect from someone who was my father's first cousin and business partner. Especially from someone who relied so heavily on my father's good will and business savvy so his lifestyle on the ranch could be preserved. I received clarity on that response years later when I was told by three separate people on three separate occasions that he was always jealous of my father.

Dad's death caused serious pain and disruption in my life, my mother's life and my sister's life. I quit my job and tried to normalize my life with Julie so we could get married and move on. I cried uncontrollably every day when I drove to the ranch. I would pull off the road and try to collect myself so I could function when I arrived. There were so many emotions that stirred within me each time I would drive to the ranch. Everyone else got to move on with their lives as normal, but mine was turned upside down. It was a mess. I didn't even know where or how to start to rebuild. Or how to begin to heal. Or what direction I should take with my life. So much was

58

thrown at me so quickly, I was literally confused about what to do next.

My mother was so depressed she shut herself in her house and wouldn't come out. Grandma and Grandpa were in a deep depression. I would go to Grandma's house every day for lunch and she and Grandpa wept. Constantly. Because their hearts were broken. And watching them, broke mine. I know how it was because I was there. Every damn day. Immersed in the pain and the sorrow and not being able to escape from it. And where was the rest of the family? I'm not sure, but I do know I was there, nearly every moment, watching them slowly die from deep within.

Shortly after dad died and before I came back full time, Joe and Jim made an executive decision to hire Joe's son-in-law and bring his family to the ranch. And the starting pay? Over 3 times what any of them had ever made per month. And not once did they consult Grandpa or me regarding this decision. And so, my position of replacing my father and running interference between Joe and Jim and Grandpa began. It was clear that neither Grandpa nor I were wanted around the ranch, but I held my ground anyway. I heard Jim say multiple times that my mother needed "to get the hell out of that house because we've got families that need to live in there". I got to listen to them ridicule Grandma and Grandpa, while embellishing the memories of their own father, who died of alcoholism because he couldn't stop drinking whiskey. All while ignoring the fact that Grandpa made it work so everyone could have a part.

On one occasion, Joe and I had finished feeding cattle in the feedlots and after we parked the equipment in the machine shed, we could hear yelling coming from the garage. We ran to see what was going on and Jim was pushing Grandpa with a 50-pound sack of cattle cake and had him pinned against the wall. I guess it made him feel like a real man, picking on an 85-year-old.

I could tell the long-term outlook was grim, so I returned to school to finish my degree while I was working full time on the ranch and taking care of Grandma and Grandpa. All while driving 50 miles in opposite directions nearly every day. 5 total semesters of a 4.0 GPA in economics and business and I graduated on my own. On the ranch, it just seemed like it was such a struggle to get along and make things work. It seemed like we just limped forward with no plan to make things better. The longer I was there the more depressing the future became. Disagreements over menial things seemed to be the norm.

During this time, on one occasion, our Veterinarian, Jim and I were working a bull with foot rot in a chute. We had the bull's leg log chained to the chute and when we were finished with him and let him go, his temper was flaring. We were pushing him back to the bull pen and Jim, with his infinite "cattle whisperer wisdom" decided he wasn't going fast enough and hit the bull with a cattle prod. The bull turned and threw Jim in the air over 8 feet and continued to maul him when he landed on the ground. The vet and I worked to get the bull off Jim and when we finally did, he lay blue and lifeless on the ground. The Vet looked at me and said, "You start CPR and I'll go call the ambulance!" And here, once again, I found myself administering CPR in the same corral where I had given it to my father just a few short years earlier. Short story is Jim broke an enormous amount of bones in his body and was in the hospital and rehab center for several weeks until he was able to return home. But he lived. The way I saw it, God had given him a new lease on life.

One morning when I walked into Grandma and Grandpa's house to say hi, as I always did, Grandma answered the door and said frantically, "Frank fell and he can't get up and I don't know why!" I ran to the bedroom and Grandpa was lying on the floor, confused, in a pool of his own urine. I talked with him and called the ambulance. He spent several days in the hospital with a urinary tract infection.

One night he was delirious and got up out of bed, pulled his catheter out and fell, breaking his elbow. He then spent time in Cheyenne Health, trying to get rehabilitated so he could return home. It was here that I spent much time with him talking about the Lord and a couple evenings before he returned home, Julie and I sat with him and he asked Jesus into his heart and accepted Him as his Lord and Savior. It was the first time I had ever seen him surrender himself to the Lord.

Even to this day, I feel that I communicated frequently with your mother to let her know what was going on. Many, many times I suggested to her that Grandma and Grandpa would not be able to stay on their own very much longer. Her response was always to just let them go as long as we could. And I respected that, even though it meant more work for Julie and me. We bought groceries for them every week because Grandma wouldn't feed Grandpa more than peaches and ice cream. We were committed to helping them keep their dignity for as long as possible.

After consulting with your mother, upon Grandpa's return from the hospital, I hired 24-hour nursing care to watch after him. I simply couldn't be there all the time. To this day, I do not know why your mother wasn't there more often. They needed her. So instead, Julie and I stood in the gap. Grandma was locking the nurses in the north room at night when I would leave and she told them to not come out. According to Grandma, the nurses didn't need to be there. Soon, it was a fruitless effort and I finally found a private nurse they both liked who could be with them each night.

Every day, you could watch Grandpa slipping. I spent countless days taking he and Grandma to Cheyenne for his doctor appointments and countless hours caring for them, all while going to school and fulfilling my responsibilities on the ranch. Those were the times when I spent hours talking with Grandpa. He told me he always wished that he had been a carpenter, but that his dad needed help on the ranch. As Grandpa digressed, Julie and I made sure they had the proper food. Grandpa wouldn't eat unless I was there to feed him. Eventually, I had to put him in Depends. And when he'd poop in his chair I'd have to clean him up and when he went to the toilet I had to hold his penis for him. Where was everyone else? Where was family? I don't know, but I was there. When people need you, you stay with them. It's as simple as that.

When I'd go to the main ranch, Jim once told me that taking care of my Grandfather was taking a lot of time away from the ranch. And Joe would tell me that he "would put him in a rest home and forget about him. He never did any good for anyone around here." I listened to this nonsense even when I knew I was working countless hours at night, upholding my responsibilities at the ranch, while the rest of them got to live their lives as usual. All the while, your mother was telling me to leave Grandma and Grandpa home and it would all be okay. She said they just needed to stay there. And even though it was wearing me down, I didn't complain and I followed through with your mother's wishes. I will probably never understand why she wasn't more available to her parents during this time.

On the first day of my last semester of school, I was in Laramie and Grandpa stepped off the step of the back door and fell on his head. I met Julie and Grandma in the emergency room in the Cheyenne hospital. It gives me chills because I can still hear Grandma sobbing. She was sobbing so uncontrollably her body was shuttering; like she knew this was the end. 62 years of marriage had culminated to this one final event. It was absolutely heartbreaking.

Once again, it was just Julie and me by their side. One final time. Decades of memories built together. Birthday parties and holidays shared together every year. Fun and laughter, playing Rummy Tile, Yahtzee and Backgammon. Memories built playing in the yard, helping in the garden and playing with kittens in the barn. Road trips in the Buick and the Cadillac and the sweet smell of Swisher Sweet cigars and wintergreen Certs. And it would all end here in this moment. Today. Since dad's death, no one seemed to care about Grandma and Grandpa anymore. And it was a sick and ugly feeling. Where was family? Where was love? Where was the respect for the two individuals who did so much for all of us? It broke my spirit. I was confused. I was hurt. And I was exhausted. It was on this day that I finally called your mother and demanded she involve herself in her parents' lives. It was too late for Grandpa, but maybe that relationship could still have meaning between her and her mother. A few days later, Grandpa passed away.

The day of Grandpa's funeral, your mother pulled Grandma out of the house where she and Grandpa had lived for 62 years. She moved her to their house in La Junta and a week or two later returned to the ranch with Grandma. Thank the Lord that Jim's wife called me and asked if I knew that your parents had brought Grandma home. Julie and I left for the ranch early the next morning and barely caught your parents and Grandma by the time we arrived. Your mother was walking in and out of the house with paintings, picture albums, and other household items and loading them into her car. I asked her what was going on and if we could just talk about things. Her response to me was this: "Nope. Our attorneys can talk." At this point, I honestly had no idea what the problem was and to this day I still don't. All I know, is for some reason, your mother developed enormous hatred for me and my only guess is because she "thinks" I took something from her. The fact of the matter is I didn't want any of it and never asked for any of it in the first place. And I never asked to be put in the position I got put in. But I fulfilled my responsibilities anyway. And I am proud of what I did and how I did it. And for that, I will not apologize for taking care of my grandparents and for faithfully fulfilling their wishes until the end.

A month after your mother moved Grandma to La Junta, she sent a bill to Grandma's trust for over $8000. I admit I was completely shocked and appalled. I had just spent over 3 years taking care of both her parents and never once charged them a dime. In fact, it never occurred to me to charge them. Why would I do that? For the next 2 months, until Grandma's passing, your mother sent a bill to the trust, for over $8000, even charging for "a sweater" she bought Grandma. Ridiculous. And shameful. But I paid the bills anyway, because I was committed to making sure Grandma's needs were met. The last thing she needed was for me to get in a big argument with her daughter, so I let it go.

Your father called me after they moved Grandma down there and said your mother was having a hard time with what Grandpa had done and to just call him at his office. So I did. And we talked, but I never got any real answers.

When Grandma died, I never heard from your mother. I learned of her death through my sister. A couple months after Grandma's death, your mother sent me an envelope. Hoping it was a letter offering how she felt and why, I opened it, only to find she had cut my head out of a good portion of family photos and decided to send me an envelope full of cut out pictures of my head. I'm not completely clear what kind of message she was trying to send, but I'm real positive it wasn't one of love and thankfulness. Had the roles been reversed, I am 100 percent damn sure my father would have never done that to you. For any reason. Ever.

Dustin, I love you and I always have. I was always excited to see you when we were growing up. I could hardly wait for you to visit so we could go play and talk. I have tremendously awesome memories of times we shared with each other and with your parents. Rides in your cool truck, riding your dune buggy on the track near your house, playing with your dog, "Duko", swimming in the Saratoga pool, family picnics in the park and playing basketball and fishing at your cabin in Riverside.

Each year I take each one of my boys on a trip of their choice and a couple years ago, Spencer wanted to go to Saratoga to go fishing down the North Platte. We booked a trip with Hack's Tackle and spent a couple days in Saratoga. I found myself showing him the places that were special to me growing up and sharing the memories of different things you and I did together. We spent time at the pool and the hot pool, sat in the river, visited the mini mart where you and I could always find cinnamon toothpicks, went to the park along the river, and went up the hill where you used to live. As I shared these memories, he asked me where you were and why we didn't hang out anymore. My response was simple and honest: "I don't know. I really just don't know."

I love your dad. He was always my favorite uncle. The times we shared at the cabin and the basketball games we'd play against him and my dad. And even though I may never understand why your mother feels about me the way she does and why she behaved the way she did, I love her too. I decided long ago that I cannot control what other people think or do.

I don't know if you'll believe a word I've said. Even if I provided you with all the documentation to prove it so, you may still react in denial and disbelief. I cannot control that. Julie and I have lived every moment of what has transpired in the last 19 years. And I can tell you, Julie and I were the only family who was there nearly every day. We know what happened, because we were immersed in every moment of it. For some reason, I have taken a lot of criticism and ridicule. I can either hold a grudge because of it or I can forgive and move on. Forgiveness doesn't mean I understand, but it means that I can give it to God and let it go. And instead of dwelling on my circumstances I can use those experiences to propel me forward to help make a difference in my own family and the lives of others who I encounter. What I have experienced as a result of Dad's death has shaped me into who I am today. And I am stronger because of it.

Unfortunately, the story doesn't end here. There's another part that needs to be told as well. And that is the story of Rabou Ranch since my father's passing. It's funny how people think they know what happened, even the people that were directly involved. Stories become embellished and small facts are left out so the truth is hard to determine. Truth is contorted because of emotion and the inability to face the facts for what they are. People believe what they want to believe. They pick and choose what can be told to benefit their own interests. Honesty and the willingness to be accountable for their own actions are thrown out, to be left and never found again. But in the end, the truth will always prevail.

Long before that day on November 4, 1999, the discussions about the ranch my father and I had were numerous. The dilemma the partners were facing is they were all close to the same age, they all wanted to slow up and they all had no money for retirement. How could this business continue to

66

exist and to supply the needs for future generations while still caring for the retirement needs of the existing partners?

By the time the mid-nineties arrived, it was a well-known fact that it took approximately 250 head of mother cows to supply the needs for one family. Rabou Ranch's numbers were about 300. But there were three families and a transition that would soon need to take affect due to the age of the partners. Thankfully, Grandpa had seen this coming almost a decade earlier and stopped drawing a wage from the ranch, allowing the other partners to pay for their life insurance policies and to draw more at the end of the year if the company had been profitable. This allowed them to begin to save for retirement but would never be fully enough to allow them to get there.

I knew from a young age that the day would come when I would return to the ranch to carry it forward. It would more than likely be after Grandpa passed away and when Joe, Jim and my father were ready to slow up. I had been groomed from an early age and had a general understanding of the operation. What I didn't know or understand were ranch finances, cash flow analysis, profitability, asset values and returns on those assets. Dad's and my discussions revolved around how to keep the ranch moving forward, provide for new generations (presumably that would be Joe's son and myself) and still provide for the retirement and benefits for the existing partners. Over the many years of these discussions, the only answer seemed to be that I would need to have an outside job or income source so things could work. And so that's what I sought.

I remember one conversation less than a year before dad's passing. I asked him when we were hunting, what would ever happen if he were to die before Joe and Jim. His answer to me was very revealing and one I never forgot. He said, "It probably won't work, but I'd like you to come back and try and then you'll have to decide what you think is best." You see,

67

my father was a realist and knew that these family businesses cannot exist into perpetuity. Virtually no business does.

When dad passed away, it set the stage for a series of events I could never have imagined. Some were the events I have already described. But that's only part of it. Now I found myself in business with my grieving Grandfather and my father's two cousins. And when dad wasn't there to be the buffer for their relationship with each other, the tides began to shift in a direction that would change the course of that business forever. The fate of Rabou Ranch was sealed. Things would have to change drastically if everyone was to continue to be involved in production agriculture.

The demise and disappearance of family farms all across our country is sad but is no surprise. The changes in the past 10 years alone have been more than many could bear. The pace of technology, the changes in how business is done and the global markets that drive the ag economy, coupled with the crippling exponential increase in ag expenses and the cost of living, all while the price of ag commodities stay the same and are driven lower. It's true that my father and certainly our grandfather, would hardly even recognize agriculture today. For those of us who have made the changes necessary to evolve our businesses as times have changed, we understand this to be the secret to long-term survival. The average age of today's farmers and ranchers is close to 60 and fewer younger people are becoming involved in production agriculture every day. The risks are simply too high and the rewards are not nearly great enough.

The longer I was at the ranch without dad's presence, the more apparent it became that I was the one who would have to invoke change in the operation if it was to survive and adequately meet the needs of all families involved. There was a chance if everyone pulled together that the integrity of the entire operation could potentially be held together as it was.

But everyone would have to change and face the inevitability of taking on some risks.

When I presented ideas about ranch expansion, I was met with opposition. Joe and Jim expressed their desire to retire and were not interested in changing things to a degree that would cause any interruption in how they had been accustomed to doing things. When I brought forth ideas of adding more cows to utilize all our grass, I was told we had enough to get by. When I brought forth ideas of leasing pastures we didn't fully utilize, I was told it was too risky. When I suggested, along with our accountant to use some of the money that had been saved over the years, to make capital purchases that could increase our cash flow, Jim was opposed because he wanted to use the money for his retirement. When Grandpa told Joe he wanted to start using some money to fix up his place, he was told sarcastically "that will never happen".

For decades, any profits the ranch made went straight to improvements on the main ranch and through years of neglect, Grandpa's place was beginning to show it. Some buildings were rotten to the point they weren't connected to the foundation. Others were leaning so far they would be difficult to ever repair. Most of the buildings were overrun with rodents because they had not been used for so many years. Additionally, the ranch fleet of equipment was aging quickly, yet there wasn't enough money to replace it when the time would come. The fleet had worked as long as it had because my dad spent countless hours in the shop fixing equipment that was 30 to 40 years old. Many parts were obsolete and had to be found in junkyards off other old equipment. He did whatever he could to make sure he kept it all running because there was no other choice.

During this time, there are a couple of events that occurred that remain in the forefront of my mind. They stand apart from all the obvious facts that there would be little to no chance of growing the operation to where everyone could live comfortably. And they even stand apart from the comments that were made about Grandma and Grandpa.

One was during wheat harvest. Joe's son-in-law and I and two of his boys had run the trucks and combines for most of harvest and one evening a rainstorm caused us to shut down. We'd been working late hours to get as much knocked out as quickly as we could. It would be too wet to harvest the next morning so I told him to take the next morning off and get some rest or spend some time with his family and we'd start the following afternoon.

When we met to get started the following afternoon, he informed me that Jim called him first thing in the morning and wanted to know where he was. He informed Jim that I had given him the morning off. Jim responded by saying, "Ron doesn't run this place, Joe and I do and when we say you need to be up here, that's what you need to do." From my perspective, this is not how partnerships work. Especially "equal" partnerships. Effective leaders lead by example and stay involved. They don't lead from their living room chair.

The second was when we had all agreed to plant some fish down on the creek. I had found a guy to buy them from and he was going to deliver them on a specific day around 10am. He didn't show for several hours and hadn't responded to my calls, but finally called me late that afternoon. He explained that he was leaving his ponds up by Laramie with the fish loaded and got stuck in his truck and had spent nearly the entire day trying to get out. He suggested still getting the fish released since they were already loaded so I agreed to wait for him at the ranch. In the meantime, I went in search of a flashlight because I knew we'd be doing a lot of the work in the dark. Grandma and Grandpa didn't have a flashlight that had any working batteries so I asked Jim if he had one I could borrow and he was glad to loan me one of his.

Later, I met the guy with the fish and we spent that evening and into the night getting the fish released at various locations along the creek. It was after 10pm when I got back to the ranch and knowing everyone around there went to bed early, I returned home to Cheyenne. Shortly after I got home, my phone rang and I saw it was Jim. That was strange because he always went to bed early and would not normally be up at this late hour. I answered right away, thinking that something must be wrong. When I answered with "Hello?" I was greeted with this response on the other end: "Where's my goddamn flashlight?" I told him I had it and brought it home with me because it was late when we finished and I would bring it out the next day. He responded by saying, "That's real nice. You loan a guy something and he doesn't even have the decency to bring it back." I apologized and the conversation ended.

I awoke at 4am the next morning and drove to the farm to meet Jim at his house just as he was getting out of bed. I informed him under no uncertain terms would I tolerate being treated that way. And having been the man that performed CPR on him a year earlier and more than likely was the one that saved his life, I remember telling him that God had given him a new lease on life, but he refused to be grateful.

Sure, I understand that in partnerships people don't always see eye to eye. But it was more than that. There were a multitude of signs that pointed to the fact that things could never be resolved. Although we could pretend to get along and continue to fight over such ridiculous things as a flashlight, things would never get any better. And now I had more than just myself to consider. Was it fair for my wife to be subjected to this kind of behavior? Was it fair to put my kids in the same position as I was thrust into?

A very good friend and mentor approached me one day at church. He could apparently see that the ranch was taking its toll on me. Having been involved with a family ranching operation earlier in his life, he encouraged me to invoke change. He had the foresight to understand that if things were rough now, they were not likely to get better over time. He introduced me to one of the top business and estate planning attorneys in the state and we began to research my options, none of which I was encouraged by. I struggled for over a year about how to resolve things harmoniously without destroying the ranch for good. Something should have been done decades before, but it hadn't and so now it rested with me to figure how to sort things out.

My options were this: 1) keep things the same and don't do anything; 2) keep my ownership and step away completely and let the others run the ranch. If I kept my interest as it was, after the death of Joe and Jim, not only would I receive a substantial amount of cash through their life insurance policies, but I would also own 100 percent of the membership interest in the ranch, allowing me to make all the business decisions, including who would work there and how profits, if any, would be split. I could not prevent them from passing their ownership interest to their family, but membership interest must be approved by the majority of remaining partners and upon the death of one of them, I would have 75 percent of that voting right. This would be a good option had I wanted a strong cash position and wanted to control the entire operation, eventually snubbing out their family's participation; 3) offer to sell my shares to them, which could only be done using the undervalued capital account numbers; 4) suggest that we divide things and each be in control of his own piece. This option required that the shares be changed and the split would be according to the agreement made after dad's passing. I would have to surrender 10 percent of what I owned and Joe and Jim would receive an additional 5 percent each. The other problem with this approach was that I could not initiate a split of this kind on my own because I didn't have a majority membership interest. If I suggested a split and they came forward with a proposal, then I could act. Otherwise, if I came forward with a proposal first, they could just ignore it and nothing would happen and family relations would more than likely be strained even further.

It took me a long time to come to terms with what ultimately needed to be done. Some days when I was working at the ranch with everyone, it was pleasant and felt okay. Other days, it was incredibly obvious that things needed to change. As I continued to mull over my options, I kept coming back to one common denominator: my children and my wife. If something were to happen to me, would it be fair to put them in the similar position I currently found myself in? The answer was always a resounding "no". I spent countless meetings with my closest mentors, numerous heartfelt conversations discussing matters with my wife, and hours praying to make the right decision. After a business has been in the family for nearly 100 years, it's not a subject to take lightly.

Over a year later, I finally concluded what to do. I would agree to split from the ranch, leaving 10 percent of everything I owned with Joe and Jim, leaving with considerably less than if I would stay. It wasn't the choice I was hoping for, but considering my options, I felt it was the best; for everyone. It was important to me to leave the operation without destroying the operation itself. I had no interest in making things difficult for the remaining partners. The risk I took was they could ignore the idea and I would be left to debate and act on one of the other options.

I developed some ideas on how the ranch could be split and how two viable businesses could be created. My initial plan was to leave what I thought would be the most important to Joe and Jim, including keeping the ranch headquarters fully intact. I would take Grandpa's and Grandma's place and the ground it sat on and a couple of other outlying pieces that would work for what I had planned for my own operation.

A big part of what made the split so emotionally taxing was that instead of talking things over and working together, they decided to make it a "me against them" fight for who got more. Weeks later, they sent back their own proposal that was, quite frankly, laughable. Suddenly what was on my side of the ledger was worth up to two times more than the same things on their side of the ledger. A very inept attempt at trying to steal even further from our family and what my father and grandfather had worked their entire lives to create. They had developed their own fictitious numbers that had no basis and were so far skewed, it left me with significantly less than the 40 percent share I was agreeing to.

I will spare you the details for now, but my original plan is essentially where we ended up. Joe and Jim, i.e. Rabou Ranch, would get to keep the main place, including my mother's house and all the facilities and buildings, 100 percent of all the livestock, all the existing mutual fund investments, all the hay and straw inventory, the existing checking account, all the accounts with our vendors, both of the main ranch brands (the Lazy DT and the Bar Cross Slash) and thus, their operation could continue to operate without interruption. We did have to value crop and livestock inventories, etc. and they had to pay me for my 40 percent share of those assets. We split the equipment according to our shares and when they asked for a piece that was on my side of the ledger, not one time did I ever refuse the request.

On my side, I was willing to compromise so we could make it work for everyone. I would be fibbing if I told you I only looked out for them. Obviously, I ultimately wanted to look out for myself and my family. But my belief is that you can do that by doing things as honestly and openly as possible. Any good agreement is good for both parties. I knew it would take compromise, and knowing them, I presumed most of the compromising would take place on my side of the table. I felt very strongly that even if I had to give some things up and walk away with less than if I were to stay, that somehow, someday, I could make it up and make it better than it had ever been.

All things considered, this sounds like a pretty smooth transaction. And really, it was. Most especially, it was incredibly seamless for the ranch. They could continue to operate with the entire cow herd, nearly all the facilities, all the haying and cattle feeding equipment, the more modern equipment and could still do it with the land that remained on their side of the ledger. Not to mention the fact that this land held most of the mineral rights in our operation because it had been in our family for so long. On my side, I would have to create another company and try to devise a plan to make it all work. I had mostly pasture, no cows, very little equipment and not near enough farmland to create positive cash flow. A very challenging task when you consider leaving behind the largest assets that provided positive cash flow and starting with 40 percent of something that didn't work very well when it was operating at 100 percent.

I really felt that the split of the ranch could be a very positive thing for everyone. If Joe and Jim wanted to retire, they had Joe's son-in-law there and he could step into their shoes. They had their houses (which incidentally don't belong to the individuals, but instead the ranch, which also means all the improvements my parents made to their house came out of their own pocket and when I left the ranch, my mother received zero), the number of cows they ran didn't change, they kept the equipment they wanted along with the place they had become accustomed to. It was very similar to what was there before the split took place.

When I approached them about splitting, I used another family in the area that had done the same thing. These family members each ended up with their own place, carried on in their own ways and still got along and helped each other when it was needed. I felt there was no reason we couldn't do the same thing. In fact, I was confident enough that I originally suggested that we keep the hunting and outfitting company we already had to continue to operate together. But was I ever wrong.

For over 6 months I still had to work on the ranch and it was difficult to say the least. Each day was a struggle. I was the last man standing on our side of the family. Through it all I learned a lot. I learned that in family ranching and farming operations when there are multiple partners, everyone develops this sense that they own it all...individually. When change is proposed, this illusion gets disrupted and causes an enormous amount of turmoil. The turmoil that is created is based on what perceptions and misinterpretations were developed when the operation was fully intact. The fact of the matter is everything changes, eventually. And it is not the changes we are to be concerned with; it is how those changes are handled and how we can make things better as a result of them.

In operations such as ours, everyone owns everything, so no one really owns anything. There is a perception that because I am part of something bigger, therefore I own it all. This could not be further from the truth. When businesses are sold or split and suddenly we can't claim to be as smart as we portrayed ourselves to be when someone else was doing all the work and there is no curtain to hide behind, reality sets in and often gives way to resentment. When things change and we must step out on our own, it becomes painfully obvious how much we really depended on keeping things together. I can assure you; it's enormously frightening to step out and start over. When things change and we step out on our own, we are left only with our own competence to perform. There's no one else to blame. And that's more than most are willing to withstand. It's much easier to stay "comfortable", wrapped in our own cacoon of safety.

I knew that if I stepped out on my own, I'd figure it out, and if I didn't, I could accept the fact that my failure rested on my shoulders, and my shoulders alone. I felt that if I left as much intact as possible for Joe and Jim and let them continue to operate as usual, they could handle it and would be able to enjoy and live the retirement they had told me so many times they wanted. What happened instead was that I was immediately ostracized, and it became a game of the Johnny Rabou family against Ron.

The rumors spread about how I took them for almost everything they had. Stories circulated about how my grandfather was (magically) rich somehow and that's the only reason I was able to move on and start over and rebuild. (This always makes me laugh because what I got from grandpa wasn't enough to even pay for half of a used tractor, let alone create and build an entire farming operation). I learned of how I had been plotting to destroy the ranch and if it weren't for them and how strong they were, they would have lost it all.

The rumors continued to spread around the community. I learned about things I had done that I never knew about. That's what small towns love! To embellish a crazy story about how some bad guy comes in and tries to destroy things, but the posse stands together and staves him off and the only reason he would ever have anything is if someone had given it to him. After all, he's just a no good, dirty rotten scoundrel. As people, we love to believe not what is true, but only what we want to believe is true. We thrive on rumors to believe that someone is really who we deep down hope he is: someone who is somehow less of a person than we are. When others have problems, even if they're fictitious, it makes us feel better about our own.

The problem with rumors is that over time, the truth begins to shine through. If the bad guy doesn't run off and instead starts to do good things, and right things, and moves forward despite what people think, perceptions start to change. They change because reality has changed. You can only call a cat a mouse for so long until finally the actions of the cat prove to you that it is just, indeed, a cat. In fact, despite what you think and what you've said, that's actually all it's ever been. The truth of the matter is things aren't always what we think they are or what we hope them to be. The problem is most of us never actually take the time or have the wisdom or insight to know and understand the difference. And maybe it's also because we don't truly want to know. If the truth is not what we hope it is, there may not be an excuse for who we are and how we live.

After the split, while the rumors spread and the animosity increased from the other side of the family, I just kept working. I worked and I planned. I worked and I educated myself. I worked and I failed. I worked and I started over. I worked and I struggled. I worked and I prayed. I worked and I never stopped. I worked countless hours, more than most would ever be able or willing to work. That's what people never see. That's because we see and believe what we want to. It's easy to justify our lack of performance and progress if we can invent excuses as to why others can become successful, but we can't. It's easy to make up stories. I call it justifiable existence.

For most it's just too hard to work. It's too hard to move forward in the face of resistance. It's hard to start over. It's hard to fail. It's hard to rebuild. It's hard to hold yourself together. It's hard to stay focused. It's hard to develop tenacity. But when I looked at myself, I decided I can do hard. And I can do work. I can do failure. I'm just stubborn enough to move forward even when the odds aren't in my favor. For the past 15 years, that's exactly what I've done. I decided that even if I lost everything, I would choose to live with courage. I would choose to move forward and use the God-given talents and abilities I was blessed with. I just needed to get out of my own way and let God lead me where He needed me to be.

After the split of the ranch was finalized, it took us a few years to figure things out. We had gotten to the point where we had spent almost everything, just trying to figure out how to make things work, but nothing seemed to come together. I finally decided I would go back to school to get a teaching degree and at least I could farm a bit in the summer. After a couple months when the course work didn't strike me as being anything I would want to spend my life doing, I decided to have a long hard look at who I was, what I wanted out of life and how I might make it work.

In my first book "Keep it Simple", I discuss in detail the process of identifying priorities in your life. This process is how I have been able to push forward with nearly every decision I make. I decided I needed to stretch my limits further and embrace more change, so I developed a business plan and acted on it. We did the unthinkable in production agriculture. Julie and I sold over 85 percent of everything we owned and we started over.

Since that time, we have built a farm where we farm more acres than our entire ranching operation used to own in total. In addition, our cattle operation spreads over several thousand more acres. We've replaced over 100 percent of the acres we once sold off to rebuild. We have rebuilt old buildings and turned them into additional sources of revenue and places to entertain and unwind. We have built modern storage facilities that allow us the flexibility to continue to diversify and expand. We have modernized and invested in technology and equipment that allow us to operate with a high level of efficiency and sophistication.

We have become experts in diversification and production. We have become experts in marketing and quality control. We have found the true value of independence. And most importantly, we have found peace. There are no more fights. No more arguments over who works harder and does more. No more pretending to own something we don't. No more hoping that if we live long enough and others die, we can one day own or run it all. No more unknowns about what happens to my wife and children when I die. This is what God intended. And what generations of people have fought and died for. Not to live life without fear, but to prosper in spite of it. To realize that we live in the greatest country and the greatest time the world has ever known. And to take that opportunity and create whatever we want to create. To live whatever life we choose to live.

I have learned that in the freest country in the world, we are surrounded by over 300 million slaves. People who are trapped mostly by their own self-imposed limitations. People who are trapped by what others think. People who are trapped because someone said they couldn't. People who are trapped by circumstances. People who do what they do because that's what they think their dead relatives would want them to do.

And let me be clear: my intention is not to be critical, nor is it to boast about what we have accomplished. The Lord has blessed us tremendously and we are humbled by His grace and the people He has put in our lives. My intention instead is to declare to others that it's okay to step out. It's okay to take some risks. It's okay to live like you want to live. It's okay to pursue your own dreams and build your own reality. My sense of purpose is clear and my responsibilities as a father and a husband are clear. My obligation as a man is to do what is right, even when it comes under fire and criticism and rumors. I do not take that lightly and I never will.

There's been a lot of water under the bridge since that blustery November day when I found myself kneeling over my father, crying and pleading for this not to be happening to me. I didn't ask for what came my way, but I accepted it. Despite my circumstances and the rumors and garbage that have tried to sidetrack us from the purpose God intended for us, we have remained true to who we are and have found blessings along every step of the way. We have not always made good decisions, but we have always found good in every decision. The key is to do something; to make things happen instead of watching things happen.

There's a lot that can be resolved when we just communicate. Our failure to do so creates confusion that can develop frustration and eventually lead to hatred. I have put the past behind me and hold no grudges to any members of our family. To this day, I remain fulfilled, enormously happy and am driven to continue to make a positive difference in this world. And I am driven to raise three little boys who will do the same. I don't know all the conversations about me that must have taken place in your family. And I don't need to know.

What I have shared with you has needed to be shared for years. When my dad and Grandpa entrusted me to run this operation, I took it very seriously. We have taken 40 percent of what was a small ranching operation that barely supported its owners, to a major farming and ranching operation that helps to make this world a better place by feeding tens of thousands of people across the globe and one that continues to grow and improve as time moves forward. It's nothing like the operation we knew in the past. It can't be, because the industry is changing too fast and the risks are too high.

Only my wife and I know how many hours, how much risk, how many sleepless nights and how much stress it has all taken. We took what was little and have transformed it into a lot. Our operation is our lifestyle. This is what we do. And I am proud to say God has provided us with multiple opportunities to make it all work and we have grabbed every single one we could, even when it seemed impossible.

I know my dad and Grandpa wanted the operation to continue, but that alone wasn't reason enough for us to move forward with it. I am most proud to say it's what we wanted too. I am proud of my heritage. I am thankful for those who came before me so that we had this opportunity. And I am humbled by what the Lord has allowed us to build.

This is our story. We will make no apologies for our accomplishments. Nor will we make apologies for how we have conducted ourselves along each step of the way. We have acted with integrity when we didn't have to. We have not acted maliciously, even though at times it would have been justifiable. We have moved forward with humility, even when it was one of the hardest things to do.

It is my hope that you may come to an understanding that what has transpired in reality was most likely not what you thought or what you were told. Please know that if your heart tells you to re-connect, we will welcome you with open arms. That has never changed. And it never will.

Frank & Dorothy Rabou, 1990

Ed Rabou, 1998

Chapter 4

FINDING CLARITY

Undoubtedly, it has been quite an adventure for us. As it turns out, we are very blessed to have been led down the road that God chose for us. It has not been the road I would have chosen, but nonetheless it's the road we were placed upon. Over the years, giving speeches, having a radio program and writing my first book, all helped me to develop clarity about my situation. And it has all helped me to develop a more defined purpose. I find that no matter where I share my story, someone who is listening can relate. We all have "stuff" that has happened to us. None of us are exempt. It has become part of my purpose to share with others, my story and what I have learned, in hopes that it will help others who are experiencing challenges in their lives as well.

After I graduated from High School, I attended the University of Wyoming and spent the next two years as a Wyoming State FFA Officer, then as a National FFA Officer Candidate. The next year I was chosen to serve as a staff member for the National FFA's "Made for Excellence" program, where we traveled across the country presenting two-day leadership seminars to high school FFA members. All these years had been a very exciting time in my life and marked the beginning of how my future seemed to begin to take shape. I later took a job with the Wyoming FFA Foundation as its director of fundraising and public relations and began to work with businesses, individuals and ag operations of all scales.

I really loved what I did and was looking forward to helping the organization and its purpose of helping students to move toward great accomplishments. And even though I was busy, I always found ways to come home and spend time with my parents and go on hunting and fishing trips with my dad. Those were the days, as a young man, that I had always hoped I would get to experience; the moments with my dad when I was an adult, not an adolescent or a child, when we could talk about the future, my dreams and aspirations and the thoughts of one day having a family and children and a successful career.

When my father passed away, the clarity I once had in my life immediately vanished. I was confused, heartbroken and lost my sense of direction and purpose. My very inner core had been damaged so severely it felt as though it could never be repaired. Trauma is an interesting thing and many of you who are reading this know exactly what I mean. While it can shake you to almost pure destruction, it can also serve as a catalyst to propel you to levels and accomplishments you never imagined possible.

When I originally left the ranch, I really had no intentions of growing our operation into what it is today. I just knew something had to change and that change would be completely dependent on my own actions. What I didn't know or understand was that when your mind is free to choose and to dream and when it is free from fighting dissention and focusing on mere existence, the world opens new opportunities for you. And it is those opportunities, if you choose to grasp them, that can positively change your life and the lives of future generations.

The first opportunity to grow my farm came my way just a couple years after I left the ranch. I had worked with the landowner of a property our ranch had been leasing for grass. When I was developing my ideas for a division, I asked him if he would be willing to lease me the hunting rights on the property separately and still lease the grass to my relatives. His response was yes, but he would prefer to lease me the grass as well. I told him I wasn't planning on keeping any cattle so it didn't make sense for me to lease the grass. He agreed and for the next couple years, I ran part of my hunting operation through the utilization of this property.

One day the landowner called me and said his family had decided they wanted to sell the property and would I know who to put him in touch with to help determine its value. I provided him with some references and told him that if he was going to sell it, I would be interested in buying it, knowing that our hunting operation depended heavily on the property. He was very glad I was interested and when he had the property appraised, we came to an agreement for its purchase.

This is a very important part of my story, as I literally did not have the resources to purchase the property. But it was an opportunity that I didn't feel like I could just let slip by. I knew the property would never pay for itself and when the family decided they also wanted to sell the house and buildings along with it, it even made less sense. Nonetheless, I figured out a way to justify its purchase. I would ask for first right of refusal on the 1100 acres of CRP that were attached to the property and if I could eventually break those acres out and farm them, I might be able to eventually make the payments. It was a risk, but I felt like it was a worthwhile one.

My next step was to flip a residential property to help make a down payment and then find a banker who bought into my idea. I was serving on a non-profit board in Cheyenne with a local bank president and when I approached him with my plan, he agreed and I was able to purchase the property. Over the next 12 years, I would also purchase all the remaining acres belonging to the family, creating a nice 1500-acre farm just over two miles from my farm headquarters.

The reason I share this story is because that purchase opened my eyes to the real possibility of growing my farm and the opportunity to create cash flow. That purchase was an enormous risk at the time and I had very little idea how I could actually pay for it. If you've been in business long enough, you understand there is very little that can be gained without saddling up with some risk. As entrepreneurs, that's what we do. Without risk, there is very little that can be gained. And, there is very little that can be learned.

As we have grown our operation since that time, it hasn't come without many sleepless nights, stressful circumstances and questions as to whether we've made the right decisions. What it has come with, however, is the knowledge that what we have created is our own and that we are in full control of how we wish to utilize those assets to add value to our operation and how we desire our operation to add value to our lives.

When we sold off our assets and started over, I determined it was time to finally look at our operation as a business rather than an heirloom. Whatever we had that didn't provide a reasonable return had to be sold. We exercised many forward and reverse 1031 exchanges during this time and we began to educate ourselves on the importance of understanding how we could utilize niche markets to continue to grow and prosper our operation.

We had to ask ourselves why we were growing what we were growing. Was it because that's what everyone else was doing or because that's what we had always done? In order to survive, we had to set aside our own beliefs about markets and crops and we began to study what was important to the consumer. In essence, we chose to be price makers in the marketplace instead of price takers. That formula has proven essential for our own survival.

Since the time of that first purchase, we have added many more acres and millions of dollars in equipment and infrastructure. We've gone from never having planted an acre of any crop, to raising a wide array of crops, including red and white wheat, peas, hay millet, proso millet, chickpeas, lentils, buckwheat, mustard, flax and corn.

We are in the organic business and we consistently work very diligently to explore and to develop new markets and opportunities and to establish and maintain positive, healthy relationships with our customers. We work hard to increase our levels of efficiency and productivity across all levels of our farm. We've developed roles within our labor force that provide our employees with a sense of ownership and pride. We've created standard operating procedures and a strong corporate structure that yield stability and consistency throughout the organization. We are in constant search for improvement and new opportunities and are willing to risk some failure in hopes of becoming better.

Recently I was interviewed on AgTalk radio where I spent a few minutes sharing our story. National Farm Journal heard the broadcast and after a series of steps and being interviewed by them directly, our farm was chosen by National Farm Journal as one of three national finalists for Top Producer of the Year. A few months later, in the summer of 2019, we were on the cover of Top Producer magazine. It was an honor that I could never have imagined. I never sought out to be recognized or to be applauded for our efforts. I was just trying to do a good job with the talents and gifts I have been given and the land I have been entrusted with. We are the first operation from Wyoming to ever have received such recognition and we are very humbled and honored to be part of such an elite and incredibly successful fraternity of production agriculturalists.

We've made a lot of mistakes along the way and I'm certain we'll make plenty more. But without risk and without failure and without heartache and leaving your comfort zone, you can never fully realize what you can do and who and what you can become.

I remember entering my father's hospital room for the last time, just before his life support was removed. I remember holding his hand, feeling his strength and leathery skin from years of working outdoors, sobbing and shaking, trying to find the words that would express my love and gratitude to such an incredible human being. As tears flooded down my cheeks, I told him I loved him and that I promised I would fulfill his legacy. And what I meant was the legacy of the farm and ranch he had spent his life building and holding together. And I meant it; whatever it took.

It wasn't until years later when I was preparing for a keynote speech that I realized that his legacy was not the ranch. My father's legacy was who he was and who he taught me to be. So many of us go through life thinking we are a failure if we can't build up some enterprise and pass it on to the next generation. Or, we feel like we are a failure if we don't stay involved in the family business or if we leave agriculture entirely. Too many times our self-worth is determined by what we do and what we have rather than by who we are. We measure our success without understanding and focusing on our intrinsic value as human beings.

There are farmers and ranchers in my community that are very driven to accumulate more and who will stop at nothing to make sure of it. They will lie, cheat nearly everyone they deal with, make up stories and start rumors to try to crush others in hopes of lifting themselves on a pedestal. While I fully realize and applaud those who have built empires through honesty, integrity and by helping to improve the lives of others, there are too many who have not. I can't help but think that their aggressive nature in seize and control is driven by an insatiable desire for power. It is, in essence, driven by egos. Until we can learn to set our egos aside, we will continue to pursue the things in life and business that only create more emptiness. We create and find fulfillment when we can truly recognize that value isn't about the accumulation of things. Instead, it is about taking our eyes off ourselves and reaching out to help others, standing strong in the face of adversity, placing relationships above money, giving God the glory for our accomplishments and blessings, and recognizing that despite how hard it may be in the moment, it is our responsibility and obligation to help make things better for the next generation. Money, property, businesses and other assets are nice but true legacies are built because of exceptional people, not because of material things.

In a world filled with hate, anger, vulgarity and such massive social and political disparity we MUST stop tearing each other down. We MUST stop living in fear. We MUST make tough choices. We MUST stand in the face of adversity and declare "I am not afraid!" We MUST decide to be a shining light and positive example to others. That's how we begin to make it better. That's how we become exceptional.

That's really all we have. There's nothing externally in this life that we get to take with us no matter how much we accumulate. It's our intrinsic value that helps to make us, others and the world a better place. And there is no amount of "I can't" that will help propel you to new heights. Have the confidence to know that you CAN make a difference. My father always told me, "Believe in yourself, believe in God and believe in what you are striving to achieve". His beliefs are reflected almost exactly in this poem by Walter D. Wintle:

> *If you think you are beaten, you are;*
> *If you think you dare not, you don't.*
> *If you'd like to win, but you think you can't,*
> *It is almost certain- you won't.*
>
> *If you think you'll lose, you've lost;*
> *For out in this world we find*
> *Success begins with a fellow's will*
> *It's all in the state of mind.*
>
> *If you think you're outclassed, you are;*

You've got to think high to rise.
You've got to be sure of yourself before
You can ever win the prize.

Life's battles don't always go
To the stronger or faster man;
But sooner or later the man who wins
Is the one who thinks he can!

It's so true, isn't it? The man who wins is the man who thinks he can. We all have a story. I'm really no different than you. We all have stuff that happens in our life. And for the most part, we can't control that "stuff". But what we can control is how we deal with it.

When we interviewed with Farm Journal for the Top Producer award, they asked me what the biggest challenge was that I had faced. My answer was not crops, prices, weather, inputs or markets. It was much different than that. My answer was perception. One of the reasons it is so difficult to make good decisions is because so many of us worry about what others will think. Until we change our thinking and determine that it doesn't actually matter what others think, we will remain paralyzed in making the proper decisions that will ultimately make positive, lasting differences for ourselves and our families. Believe me, I know this firsthand.

I knew that by leaving the ranch, not only would I lose a big portion of what I owned, I would more than likely be perceived as a terrible human being by others in our community and our family. But I don't live for those people. They don't pay my bills, they don't love my children and my wife, and I do not live my life to seek their approval. I do not care what they think; I can't. But I didn't always feel that way, especially in the beginning. What neighbors and family members said about us hurt initially. And I could not understand why some people never wanted to hear my side of the story. But 20 years later I know. If you hear the other side of the story, you just might discover that you're wrong. And that's more than most people can bear. It would take away their excuses for why they are the way they are. There will always be those who don't want to see you succeed.

WHAT MATTERS?

Because it is always a hot topic of discussion, I find it important to mention the subject of money. It is very easy to measure one's success monetarily because that is an easy means of measurement. Land, equipment, cattle, cash in the bank, etc. are all measurable items. While this is a standard means of measurement for the world, be careful not to get caught up in the game of "I have more things than you do". Stepping out and making your own way doesn't necessarily have to be about making more and having more; what it's really about is *being more*. It's about creating peace and harmony in your own life and creating your own destiny. And as in my case, it's about laying the groundwork so your children are not subjected to the turmoil, stress and disharmony that gets exponentially worse with the passing of each generation.

You will make yourself crazy if the only thing you can focus on is the economic side of the equation. There are many people in this world who have a lot monetarily, but it doesn't mean they are better off. Many, especially the ones who have never actually had to earn what they have, are still empty inside. They'll buy new tractors, new trucks, more land, add on to their house and go on vacations, but just having more money doesn't magically change who they really are inside.

Many farm and ranch operations are funded outside of agriculture, whether it is from old money, rich relatives, oil and gas, minerals or outside investors. While that is great for those operations, if you're like me, that was something I've never been able to depend on. I am not criticizing, but merely pointing out that this type of "success" rarely has anything to do with ambition, creativity, innovation, improvement, hard work, intelligence, risk, ability or vision. It is often just luck; nothing more. These outside revenue streams can be a wonderful thing for farms and ranches and have allowed many operations to continue for generations and to expand and improve. But still, the vast majority of farms and ranches have had no such luck. How are they also to survive?

I can assure you through personal experience that even in tough times and even without these outside revenue sources, it is completely possible to change, grow and thrive. I am very proud of the fact that we have built our operation through creativity and innovation, risk and careful planning. And we have done it all through production agriculture and the work we put into what we do every day. I'm sure the golden goose would be great, but for us, I never have to worry about what happens if the goose is no longer there. We'll figure it out no matter what we do or where we go. No golden goose required.

Don't ever think you can't succeed because you are just not as "lucky" as your neighbor. It might not always feel like it, but there are enormous benefits to creating value on your own versus having it handed to you. Outside revenues can make anyone look like a smart businessperson. Just take the God-given talents and abilities you have been blessed with and go make the absolute best of them. Push yourself each day to be more, not just to have more. In the end, who you are is what really matters. Is the world a better place because you are in it? Are others better people because they know you? Think of the words that William Hersey Davis wrote so eloquently:

The circumstances amid which you live determine
your reputation;
The truth you believe determines your character.

Reputation is what you are supposed to be;
Character is what you are.

Reputation is the photograph;
Character is the face.

Reputation comes over one from without;
Character grows up from within.

Reputation is what you have when you come to a
new community;
Character is what you have when you go away.

Your reputation is learned in an hour;
Your character does not come to light for a year.

Reputation is made in a moment;
Character is built in a lifetime.

Reputation grows like a mushroom;
Character grows like the oak.

A single newspaper report gives you your reputation;
A life of toil gives you your character.

Reputation makes you rich or makes you poor;
Character makes you happy or makes you miserable.

Reputation is what men say about you on your tombstone;
Character is what angels say about you before the throne of God.

KEEPING PERSPECTIVE

What I have learned is all the money in the world doesn't make you a better person, it just makes you a richer one. There's no price you can put on freedom of soul and mind. And all the money in the world will not fix the many challenges, regrets or circumstances that are part of all our lives. No amount of money could lure me back to be in the environment I found myself in when my dad passed away. But that doesn't mean I don't sometimes wish some things could have remained the same. There's a lot of things I wish; like that my dad would have not died when he did; that he and I could have conversations about life; that my grandparents were still here; that everyone in our family could just talk to each other and love each other.

Change is hard; I get it. And sometimes it just flat stinks. But keep perspective on what you are doing and why you are doing it. The world isn't a level playing field. There's a lot you can't control so stay in control of the things you can. Make the best decisions you can with the information you have at the time. Be confident in who you are. Focus on what is important.

You may feel, as I did, that you have been wronged or that your family was wronged, or that the situation you find yourself in is completely unjust. You're probably right on all accounts. But keep this in mind; in the Bible, Matthew 5:44-45 says this: "But I say, love your enemies! Pray for those who persecute you! In that way, you will be acting as true children of your Father in heaven. For He gives His sunlight to both the evil and the good, and He sends rain on the just and the unjust alike." Things can seem enormously unfair. And they may very well be. But don't let that prevent you from doing what is ultimately still right for you and your family. In the end, we take nothing with us and all we think we "own" is owned only by the Creator. It all belongs to Him.

I don't consider my story to be an anomaly. It's just the one I know. Many of you have stories that are far more compelling than mine and you've had far more difficult challenges to deal with. As you have read, it has probably become evident that I was upset with the way things were handled directly after the death of my father and for many years afterward. But I know my partners were upset too. I want to be clear that I should not be exempt from criticism because we all know there are always two sides to every story. My goal in sharing my story is not to shed negative light on the ranch or the people still involved with it. In telling my story and reiterating it in parts, I want to be as honest and forthright as possible and I want to share as much information as reasonable in hopes of providing clarity and an understanding of the correspondence that actually transpired, all without the personal bias. Perhaps some of the documentation I have revealed will provide valuable insight as you consider your own options. While I always acted with good intentions, those intentions at times, could have been taken as malicious. Without a doubt, both sides would tell you that something absolutely needed to be done, although the process and results may not have been perfect or what any of us would have chosen. In a perfect world, each partner would own it all and keep it all.

My intention in sharing my story is not to magnify the fact that splitting a family business is extremely difficult and upsetting. Rather, it is that I hope there is some part of my story that reaches out and relates to you. It's likely that something similar has happened or is currently happening in your family too. Sometimes we just need to know that someone else has experienced what we're going through. We need to know we're not alone. We need to know that it will all eventually work out. We need to know that in the end it will all be okay.

While you are in the process of trying to figure out what to do and what is right for your family, it's pretty easy to get engulfed in the emotional drama and trauma that ensues. For a time, it may so fully consume you that you are barely able to see or understand anything beyond it. In my situation, was I angry and upset? Absolutely. Did I feel cheated and ostracized? Absolutely. Did I complain because things just didn't seem fair? Absolutely. Those were all real stumbling blocks for me when I finally chose to leave. But I finally had to decide that, Lord willing, I would figure out how to make it all work. I felt as if I had no other choice. Everything I was about to embark upon was completely uncharted territory. And once that journey began, I literally had no idea where I might end up.

As your own story is unfolding, keep in mind that the worst thing you can do is to continue to hang on to resentment, no matter how ugly things have gotten or might get. I knew it was not in my power to change what had taken place. But what was in my power was to forgive and to move on. If I was to ever fulfill my purpose and to live my own life, I had to. Release the resentment, forgive others for what they have done, don't look back and keep moving forward. It's an absolute necessity if you ever want to find peace.

The bottom line is this: agree or disagree with each other, hate or love each other, in the end you are all still family and more than likely still members of the same community. That's one of the hardest parts about any kind of family operation; we don't get to choose our partners and because of that, great dissention often develops. But what we can choose is how to work things out amicably and to ultimately love and care for each other in the end.

Many of my cousins are living productive lives and are raising great families. One of them is one of my very best friends. And now because the ranch no longer serves as a wedge between us, we can all love and appreciate each other for who we are as people. It's taken some time, but with each passing year, some of those relationships are gaining strength. We all have things we could continue to be upset about. I have cousins that were never even allowed an opportunity to become involved, even if it was maybe what they had wanted more than anything. If you hold onto resentment and never extinguish the past, it will eventually destroy who you were ultimately created to be.

Several years ago, I asked the wife of my only living previous partner if they would be willing to just sit down and talk. Her response was, "Nope! We are not interested!" I literally don't understand that, but if they ever change their mind, I would be willing to have a conversation and gladly welcome them into my home. For me, though there were truly tumultuous times when I couldn't stand being around who I was in business with, it was never about creating such divisiveness that we couldn't all still get along. As part of finding clarity, I have come to understand that the individuals weren't so much what I disliked, but rather the situation at hand was what was sometimes completely unbearable. At the same time, I have also developed the understanding that some people are just plain disagreeable and unless they get 100 percent of their own way all the time, they will always be cantankerous and always make everything someone else's fault. Plain and simple, they are who they are and nothing you can do will ever change that.

I tell my children that the right kind of leadership is hard. Standing up for what's right and standing firmly in your beliefs is not easy. But it is absolutely necessary. Just look at the world we live in. So many who are in leadership positions change their opinions based on which way the wind is blowing. Opinions are changed depending on who is affected and where the money comes from.

About 22 years ago, the Prebles Meadow Jumping Mouse was a big topic of discussion in our area. When I read about it, I couldn't help but write a letter to the editor of the newspaper who had printed the article. It seemed, as the article had described, that condemning thousands of acres of farmland because of the possibility of the presence of a mouse was absurd. And the irony of the whole thing was that the mouse had to be killed to measure its skull to determine if it was, indeed, this species. In rebuttal to my letter, a lady from a local nature group replied, pointing out the importance of the diversity to the ecosystem that this mouse contributed. To my recollection, her general argument was that agriculture was destroying certain species and that it was okay to condemn the areas in which this creature was found.

I couldn't just leave her comments without response so I wrote another letter in return. My letter stated that I accepted her argument, but only under the following condition: we would also do research in her neighborhood and if the possibility existed the mouse could be found there, her house would be condemned without the possibility of her living there or selling it for any reason. She wrote back and stated that my argument was not valid because it was not the same thing. Of course it isn't, I would argue, because now it affects her.

My point is that it is very easy to have an opinion about something that doesn't directly affect you. It's easy to be an expert about something you've never experienced. It's easy to look from the outside and offer suggestions about how others need to live their lives. But when it affects you, it's different. It changes what you think, what you do and what you believe. It changes your perception. And that perception is everything.

We are at a pivotal point in America where we need leaders to stand strong and to stand in the gap for what is right and for what is just. We need people who will make the right decisions, even if it's hard and even if they take a lot of criticism for it. We need leaders with strength of character, leaders with strength of mind, leaders with wisdom and non-selfish agendas, leaders who stand in the gap for those who won't or can't stand up for themselves.

In the course of the past 20 years, I have discovered that the naysayers never change. They believe what they want to believe and they always will. I learned that leadership is not about me. It's about doing what is right. It's about understanding what is best for future generations that I will never meet. And it's about acting in the face of fear, not in its absence. When you step out and make good decisions and move your life forward for the right reasons and do not act with malicious intentions toward others, you can truly make a difference.

One of the joys in my life is to travel this great country and speak to audiences about my experiences and to tell my story. And as a result, I have found we are much more alike than we are different. People sometimes need the confidence to know that if someone else has done something and succeeded, they can too. The situation I was faced with upon my father's death is not necessarily unusual. It is a story that permeates and infects American agriculture today and it's something we need to address. We need to talk about solutions.

Chapter 5

DEVELOPING FOCUS

Lewis Carroll, famous author of "Alice's Adventures in Wonderland", wrote "If you don't know where you are going, then any road will take you there." I usually just say "If you don't know where you're going, any path will do." The greater point here is that without focus and direction, you just might end up somewhere you never wanted to be. Stop a moment to think about why you are doing what you are doing. Then ask yourself if this is really where you want to be. If it truly isn't then take a step in a different direction. If you put your best foot forward and intentionally work to make things better, then that's exactly what they'll be. I understand very well the fears of venturing into unknown territory. It's extremely scary so don't just start wandering down a path aimlessly. Intentionally choose the path in which to go based on who you want to become and what you want to accomplish. Choose your OWN way.

To begin the journey of making your own way, there are some key points to address the concerns for those who are involved in family businesses and production agriculture. There are three common themes I discuss when I speak to audiences across our country. They are relationships, communication and trust.

RELATIONSHIPS

First, relationships. Relationships are the foundation of who we are. We seek them. Some of us find negative ones to replace the ones we hope to someday have or the ones we remember in days gone by. Some of us find positive ones and understand what it takes to keep them that way. We all seek approval in one form or another. For many of us, the relationships we seek are in our family. For others, it's outside of the family. But the key to any relationship is to recognize whether they are healthy.

In my case, I have very positive and healthy relationships with mentors and friends who are outside of my family. I also have a very positive, healthy relationship with my immediate family. The relationships I once had with members inside the ranching side of the family existed, but I could always tell they were conditional. If things went their way and I was of use to them, those relationships would remain intact. But if I were to ever disagree or go my own way, they would cease to exist. Even at my young age I knew that. I could sense that as soon as I went against the grain, I would turn from friend to foe and those relationships would end. We all have these relationships in our lives and we all, for the most part, know who they are with.

I would first challenge you to look at the relationships you have in your life and be honest with yourself about their health and necessity. Sometimes we stay in relationships because we just don't want to say no. To be clear, I am not advocating going around and destroying the relationships in your life because they are making you unhappy. What I am advocating, however, is to evaluate each and its own contribution to your health and well-being. It doesn't mean you can't still be nice to these folks, but it does mean you need to control and monitor these with caution so they don't continue to take you on an emotional roller coaster. If you are spending a majority of your time putting out fires that others are causing in your life and constantly having to hold back your true identity and your beliefs, then that leaves very little time for you to work on how to productively move forward in your life and to improve yourself and the positive healthy relationships that have actual meaning.

One of the more difficult times I had in dealing with relationships over the past 20 years was with my father's sister. I grew up knowing my aunt and uncle and my cousin very well. We did a lot together and I always thought that relationship had significant meaning and was important to all of us. But when my father died, that relationship changed forever. I'm not sure exactly why, but there was no doubt her actions came as a complete surprise to me. She no longer took interest in our family or in my grandparents. The change was so swift and so sudden it was almost hard to believe. How could someone who you knew for so long and who you thought you knew so well, change so drastically? It was hurtful to me when my aunt wouldn't spend time with her own parents and I know it was most especially hurtful to them. During the process of caring for my grandparents I tried my best to make sure she was informed and included in the decisions that needed to be made. It was very hard for me to picture myself completely disengaging from my aging parents' lives like she was doing with hers.

When my grandfather passed away, the situation turned for the worse. And when she pulled my grandmother from her home and attempted to take as much as possible from my grandmother's trust, I still found myself trying to communicate and work with her. I spent a lot of time trying to get her to see things from a logical perspective.

The following letter I sent to her on December 20, 2002 appropriately describes my tone and approach to her behavior after she billed her mother's trust for over $8000 so she could be paid to care for her own mother:

"Dear Aunt Lizzy:

I have received the information that you have sent to your attorney as well as the letter you sent to me on December 3, 2002. After much consideration and research, I have developed a solution that I feel will not only meet Grandma's needs but will also fairly compensate you for your time and effort in caring for your mother. Let it be noted that there is an additional party, besides Grandma, you and myself, who has a very vested interest involving the decisions that are made now and in the future. Since she is also a beneficiary, I have contacted Wendy [my sister] and discussed my decision with her. She feels that this decision is quite fair and supports it 100 percent.

I have spent time researching assisted living facilities that would provide comparable services for Grandma if you were unable to care for her. These facilities charge a monthly fee that includes all the following: three meals per day; all snacks; all utilities including cable television but excluding telephone; transportation; and activities both within the facility and in the community. Rental rooms include a kitchenette, living room, bedroom and bathroom. According to sources, the national average for assisted living is $60 to $70 per day. The average of $65 per day for 30 days equals $1950. As a result, keeping the best interests of everyone involved, my decision is as follows:

You will be provided a monthly stipend for providing housing, transportation, activities, snacks, meals, and all utilities (including telephone). This amount will be $1950 per month.

In the past, Grandma was receiving slightly over $550 per month for social security. She used this money for herself and for other people, including any types of donations that were given by her and Grandpa. In order to prevent the diminishment of the lifestyle that Grandma is accustomed to, the amount that she will be allowed for herself each month will continue to be $550.

The total of these two amounts equals $2500 per month. Following the recommendations from bank trust departments and legal counsel, the first $1600 of this amount will be taken from Grandma's social security. You will need to handle the management of this money with Grandma. An additional check compensating for the difference of $900 will be sent personally to you at the end of each month.

Additionally, the trust will provide the subsequent benefits for Grandma: 1) payment of all necessary medical expenses; 2) payment of income taxes and preparation of tax returns; 3) payment of insurance and license fees for the brown 1989 Ford F-150 pick-up; and 4) payment of personal property insurance.

The following items will be mutually understood: 1) I will file Grandma's tax return and handle all necessary preparations and payments just as I have done for the last 3 years; 2) necessary medical bills will be itemized by you and sent to me for payment; 3) according to quotes that I have received, the annual premium for personal property insurance should not exceed $150; 4) no unnecessary or additional expenses of any kind will be paid by the trust unless they are first agreed upon by you and I.

The insurance on the brown pick-up will expire on January 26th. Since Grandma is not a driver of the pick-up, the ranch insurance company requires that she be removed from the policy. You will need to add the truck to your own insurance policy before January 26th and can submit the bill to the trust. I would recommend a policy that covers liability with limits of 100,000/300,000. If you feel so inclined, comprehensive insurance may also be included. Furthermore, I would suggest a deductible of $500. In addition, if you would like to transfer the title of the truck into your name, Wendy and I will agree to that and will then sell the Cadillac and split the proceeds between the two of us.

Next, I would like to address the issue of Grandma's and Grandpa's will and trust. Both trusts were originally formed when Grandma and Grandpa were very capable of making thorough and equitable decisions. Grandma's trust was formed on June 27, 1995 and Grandpa's trust was formed on January 31, 1990. Both trusts say the same thing and the only thing different between the two was the ownership of Grandpa's share in the ranch, which was included in his trust.

Historically, the ranch partners only wanted to pass the ranch to male members of the family to prevent potential splitting of the operation because of distant in-laws that may otherwise become involved. Though some may not agree with the structure of the agreements for the company, nonetheless, we are all bound to decisions that were made many, many years ago.

When the trusts were originally created, both you and Dad were given equal consideration and shares of the assets outside of the ranch that Grandma and Grandpa owned. Upon the death of Grandma and Grandpa, you and Dad were to share equally the assets in the two trusts. If Dad was not living at that time, his share of assets was to be transferred to his children and if they were not living, these assets were to be transferred to his children's descendants. If you were not living when Grandma and Grandpa passed, your shares were to move to your child and if he was not living, your half was to be passed to your child's descendants.

After Dad's passing, an amendment was made to the trust stating the changes that were required. Exactly following the provisions in the trust, as descendants of dad, Wendy and I were listed as the next beneficiaries in line for his portion. The other half, of course, remains in your name and if you were to pass before Grandma, your son would be given the exact same treatment as Wendy and I. Grandma and Grandpa were extremely wise to *make sure that either their children or their children's descendants were treated equally.*

After Dad's passing, I have ensured that Grandma's and Grandpa's wishes were fulfilled. Even though you were not around to take care of your parents after Dad's death, I have made it a point that you were treated fairly, according to the way that Grandma and Grandpa had requested. I do not believe they could have treated their children or their children's families more equally.

In addition, after Dad's death, I was appointed as trustee to care for Grandma's and Grandpa's financial needs. I have successfully performed this responsibility and have also provided moral support and interacted with them daily since Dad's death. The last several months, I cared for Grandpa so he could stay at home despite his worsening condition. My care included that which was so personal, that I know it was very embarrassing for him. May you be reminded that I performed this care while working full time, driving 100 miles each day, attending school, speaking around the state, and remaining active in community service. Even though I could have refused this care and demanded that you take care of your father, I did not complain and stepped way above my call of duty as a grandson.

In closing, I am including a check for $2250 for the other half of October ($450) and the months of November ($900) and December ($900). As I mentioned earlier, I will send the next check at the end of January. If you have any questions, please don't hesitate to contact me."

It was within just a few months of this correspondence when my aunt sent me an envelope full of cut-out pictures of my head from the family photos. I never will forget the shock when I opened the envelope and looked at what was inside. I'm 100 percent positive even my 8-year-old wouldn't respond to someone in this way, so it came as a complete surprise when it came from my aunt, who was then around 60 years old. It truly was a disgraceful act on her part.

The reason I wanted to include this correspondence to her and specifically touch again on this story is because relationships are the single most important thing we have when dealing with issues in our lives. Every relationship serves one of two purposes. One, they provide a positive influence in our lives that provide a positive interaction and encouragement that help to propel us into a purposeful existence; or two, they tear us down, leave us questioning our own competence and leave us closer to living in fear and negative self-consciousness.

I've said this already, but if you want to move forward in your life, you must recognize the folks who are building you up and the ones who are tearing you down. And when you do, you must "clean house" and rid yourself of the relational parasites who are leaving you confused and frustrated. In addition, I have learned it is a futile effort to try to convince these folks to see things other than the way they choose to see them. There are no amounts of truth, facts, logical thought processes or obvious circumstances that will change their minds. They are the irrational and unreasonable people I spoke about earlier in the book. People develop their own realities based on their own perceptions, whether there is any truth to those perceptions or not.

It is imperative that you stand strong, speak the truth and do what is right, even in the face of resistance. My aunt was acting so irrationally, it became necessary that I act swiftly and respond clearly to her behavior. Leadership is not about popularity. It is about serving others and doing what is right no matter how difficult it may be. In my position of trustee it was my job to act responsibly and reasonably and to be clear about my expectations, regardless of my aunt's perceptions.

In my view, it should be obvious that my old ranch partners and my aunt should thank me for giving them more and allowing them the opportunity to move

117

forward with their own lives without having to have been inconvenienced. It makes no sense to me why they are the way they are and why they have not responded with love, grace and thankfulness. But it's not my job to make sense of it. It's my job, as a human being, a father, a husband, a friend, a business owner, a community member and as a leader to continue to make the right decisions no matter what others think. What they think has absolutely no bearing on who I am or where I am going.

For most of us, this battle of relationships and perceptions of others prevents us from becoming who we are truly meant to be. People will do what they want to do, but only if they want to do it bad enough. For most, they talk about breaking out. They talk about making change. They talk about becoming more. They talk about when the time is right. They talk about when their circumstances change. They talk, talk, talk. And they follow with no action; just excuses.

I've had lots of people and even close friends tell me that they could never do what I did. Not because they can't do it, but because they won't. They say, "My situation is different. That would never work for me."; or "There's too many people involved in our operation and I'm just a small shareholder. Just that alone doesn't allow me to make any changes."; or "It's not that bad, I'll just continue to go with the flow and it will all work out."; "I keep saying we need to change things, but no one will listen to me, so I can't say I didn't try." Not words of wisdom or conviction, for sure. Just reasons that justify never having to get uncomfortable and change. Reasons that don't require action, ambition or vision. Reasons that don't require strength, tenacity or risk. Don't waste your time trying to convince or justify to others who you are or why you are doing what you are doing. Just go do it. Develop selective hearing and grant attention to only the people, places and things that really matter in your life. And as you move forward and make progress and as you change your circumstances and your life and your future, those folks will say to you what they've said to me. "You're just lucky." "Yep", I say. "I sure am."

COMMUNICATION

Second, communication. Communication is a building block to positive, healthy relationships. Without honest, open communication there will always be problems. Those problems may not surface right away, but they will undoubtedly surface at some point. The problem with communication is most of us think we are great communicators, but we are not. One of my favorite activities to do as a trainer is to highlight this fact. People are always shocked to learn that they are not as effective with communication as they thought. Most of us think that because we are talking, we are good communicators. We think that because others are listening to us, we must be making sense to them.

I was recently part of a discussion where someone asked my opinion about a certain topic. As I was forming my thoughts as I spoke while trying to make my response sensible enough to understand, there was another person in the room who kept finishing my sentences for me and interjecting his opinions before I could even finish my own thoughts. It was truly annoying. The person who kept interjecting didn't actually have experience regarding the subject, but wants to, so by making his own suggestions, he was validating his own desire for authority and expertise. Meanwhile, my response was diminished because I could not fully engage the person asking the question because of the interference.

Whenever I get asked a question, rather than just responding with all my "profoundness", I like to ask further questions of the other party so I can more thoroughly understand where the individual is coming from and can provide the best response possible. Just because you are talking, doesn't mean you are communicating. And when you do talk, you might be diluting the information that needs to be communicated.

A major portion of effective communication is not talking, but rather, listening. The problem with listening is we all have different styles in which we listen. What someone else says isn't always what we hear. And often, what is meant by one individual is completely misconstrued by another. One of the best methods for advancing your family business forward is to openly communicate. Sit down together with your business partners and be honest about what you see as the future of the business and your personal role in that future. And let your partners speak without interruption. This process is no time for you to interject your opinions about their input. If you don't think it will go well or you don't want to initiate the conversation yourself, talk to your attorney, accountant or a mediation expert to see if they will call the meeting and help to mediate the discussion. A great option to help your family and business move forward is to hire an ag consultant. It's not as important how you start, just as long as you do. And don't kid yourself; that is much easier said than done. But you must start somewhere and that is a great starting point.

Ask your partners and other family members what their vision is and what role they want to play. Be honest with each other about the comfort level of the role you are currently playing. Does it play to your strengths? Are you in that role just because no one else wants to be? Are you satisfied with the current structure of the business? Do you see other ideas for expansion and improvement? If a generational change is on the horizon, are you preparing for it properly? How do you know? Have you given the next generation an opportunity to provide input and insight? A good consultant can initiate this discussion and help you navigate family dynamics and create a solid, efficient and unbiased corporate structure that will help to protect the integrity and functionality of both the family and the business.

Most times, we don't ask tough questions and have hard conversations because we are afraid of the answers. But what we must realize is just because we don't talk about them and bring them to the surface, doesn't mean the issues aren't there. Doing nothing is still doing something. But that something will become bigger and bigger over time, until it gets to the point where our operation did and things had to change drastically. Failing to communicate may seem like the right thing to do for a long time, but eventually this failure will cause massive disruption in the family and in the business.

One of the problems in our family operation was failing to communicate openly and honestly with each other. For decades, our farm operated under the "sons only" provision I described earlier. Although I can believe my father and my grandfather may have been comfortable with it, I can't imagine at least one of the other partners was okay with it. He only had one daughter and that provision automatically disqualified her from ever being a partner in the operation. I'm not saying she was, but what if she was more qualified than any other heir? In our case, it wouldn't have mattered. What about the other partner who had only one son and three daughters, the son showing the least interest in the ranching operation of all four siblings?

Had all the partners sat down and been honest with each other, rather than just accepting things for what they were, changing that provision would have ultimately led to the retention of my side of the family's entire share. If all the partners had discussed generational transfer and the future of the operation, perhaps an amicable split would have taken place and each side of the family could have set out to control their own interests and as a result, created the future they felt best suited their own individual needs. That conversation would have been much easier to have because three of the partners were all from the same generation. But when my father was no longer there, it created instant divisiveness between all three generations. My father's two cousins resented my grandfather, wanted control and wanted to retire; my grandfather was risk averse and felt cut out by his nephews; and I was interested in growth and progress but found my time being spent playing the middle man to keep the peace, knowing full well that it was not a winning position, it was a true downhill spiral, only to be remedied by full cyclonic change.

TRUST

Third, trust. Trust cannot exist without a positive healthy relationship and open and honest communication. They are all synonymous with one another. Relationships matter. Communication is imperative. Trust is everything. Without trust, nothing will work. If you are constantly looking over your shoulder wondering where your business partners stand or have side conversations about what you think is going on or what you think will happen in the future, that is a sure recipe for disaster. Think of it this way; if you are married and your wife is wondering if you are sneaking around every time you leave the house, what does that do to the health of your relationship? If you don't openly and honestly communicate with her and let her know your concerns and thoughts, whether they have any basis or legitimacy at all, they will poison your relationship. Her trust in you is eroded and your relationship with each other becomes filled with friction. Ignoring what you feel or ignoring your concerns doesn't cause them to go away. They will always be there until you take it upon yourself to take action to fix them.

The question in your mind may be, "what if there is no trust to begin with when it comes to the relationship with your business partners?" I understand. That's where I was. Numerous times I communicated to them what I was feeling and shared my ideas of how we could grow and prosper our business, but my thoughts fell on deaf ears. We came from such opposite ends of the spectrum, what we needed to overcome seemed insurmountable.

At the time, had I known about the possibility of hiring a consultant who understood the intricacies of the various dynamics and how to make sense of them all, it is possible we could have retained the integrity of the entire business.

It is also entirely possible that our problem could not have been solved because our differences were so stark. By the time we reached the breaking point, too much water had passed under the bridge. This was evident in their response to me when I came to them with the idea of splitting the ranch.

My initial idea didn't involve us never again working with each other. It didn't even involve us fundamentally changing everything. In fact, it offered only that we split assets so we all knew what we had, along with the idea that we could still help each other and function together yet remain independent. For the position I was in, I felt that to be a non-threatening, reasonable and appropriate way to initiate the discussion. When my partners responded to this idea, they took such offense to it, they intentionally sought out to seemingly steal as much from my share as they possibly could. I really felt we could have a discussion and work things out, but their response unfortunately told me they had no interest in preserving relationships or the integrity of our family operation.

I don't have any profound answer or piece of great wisdom I can share in dealing with this. My only advice is that some people are just plain irrational and unreasonable. And those are the people you should stay clear of being in business with, whether they are part of your family or not. No matter how you approach them, you will be wrong and you will be the bad guy. But don't spare yourself the opportunity to deal with them anyway. Deal with them now so your children or your grandchildren or your spouse won't have to. Develop a plan that you believe will best suit your future needs and the needs of your family and stick to it. Stay firm, hold your ground and don't be fooled or manipulated into deviating from it.

Chapter 6

DISCOVERING SOLUTIONS

I always told folks that if they knew both sides of the story, they might be surprised what really did happen. And I've always said that when it came down to it, I would always be as open as possible in showing others the details of what transpired if they were ever interested in learning for themselves. In the following pages, I will unveil some of the documents that began the discussion of the split and what resulted from it. As you review this material, my hope is it will provoke thought about your own situation.

In October of 2003, I called an in-person meeting with my partners. Although I was more than 30 years younger, I presented them with my ideas on how I thought it was time we look at dividing things so we all knew where we stood moving forward. That was a form of action. For years, they had both told me they wanted to retire and on several occasions, one of the partners told me he wished they would have split the place years earlier so he had full control of what he owned and could use it to help himself financially in his retirement years. From the time I had become a partner, we had discussions as a group of how to best move forward. Some, I had set up with our accountant so he could help mediate the discussion. It was clear my partners were interested in retirement and one even went as far to say that the money we had in the bank should be used to help fund his retirement. I was, of course, interested in investing capital to create more revenue.

As I mentioned in the correspondence to my cousin, the management of our one employee was even an issue. Since he was the son-in-law of one of the partners, that partner was not interested in anyone else managing him except himself. As a result, he continued to perform menial tasks to fill time rather than performing tasks that could advance the productivity and growth of our operation. His tasks included spending weeks building gates that we could have purchased for pennies on the dollar once the materials and his labor were calculated. And tasks like spending time straightening used nails and staples with a hammer and vise. Tasks like that made me crazy and I had no voice in the matter whatsoever.

After one of the partners informed me that I needed to be outside working more, I went as far as breaking out each partner's job description so we could be sure we were sharing the workload at least somewhat equally and so we each had a definitive description of what we were in charge of. When I met with him at his home after his afternoon nap (literally!), it was clear we were not. My job description was two pages longer. If you have spent your life strictly as a laborer, then that's what you understand. You can't see, because you don't know, what all is involved in running a business. It's much more than sitting in the truck feeding cows, although that is important too. But I was also sure that wasn't a three, let alone, four-person job. If you're a businessperson of any kind, you know and understand the difference between busy work and productive work. He also told me in the same discussion that I shouldn't be involved in anything else. "That's what killed your dad", he said. "Just stay here on the ranch and work with us guys and it'll give you everything you need." True, if mere existence was high on my list. But it wasn't. It was clear the battle was lost before it had even begun. There were just too many obvious signs of irreconcilable differences. Our perspectives were just too far apart.

After two years of meetings with my partners, both with and without outside mediation and direction, it was clear we were at a standstill. I took it upon myself, in the terms of both time and finances, to take action and spent a year trying to figure out how to resolve the numerous issues we faced. I met with a highly qualified and experienced estate lawyer and we reviewed option after option. My goal was that we could all remain civil with each other and still work to help each other, all while having separate operations and knowing who owned what. Afterall, why couldn't my partners, who were primarily interested in running cattle, lease my pasture to run their cattle operation and I could lease their farmland? The resources would remain intact, we would just be specializing in what interested each side of the family and operating our entities independently.

Once I had finally arrived at a conclusion of how to accomplish this and put together what I thought would be an excellent and very fair start to the discussion, I called a meeting and we met in one of the partner's homes. It would be the last day he ever spoke to me. Because of the reaction from my partners, the situation only escalated from this point. Here are the exact words in the document I presented to them. I have not shown the numbers to retain the privacy of all involved:

"I am providing you with documents that describe a possible way that we could dissolve Rabou Ranch, LLC and allow each family its own right to control their portion of the LLC assets. I am finding the current situation unworkable and I believe it is disadvantageous to all of us at present. As things now stand, none of us has complete control over any of the company assets, nor can any member receive the full benefit of his ownership portion. In the current situation there are two members who each own a 25 percent membership interest and are reaching retirement age. All the members seem to have differing goals and places they would like to be in their own lives. One member controls 50 percent membership interest and would have 100 percent control following the death of the two older members. A fair arrangement might be for the LLC to be dissolved and each member can then have control over his share of the company assets and be able to pass on the control rights to future generations rather than have control monopolized by the descendants of whichever of the three current members is the last to die.

The documents and lists that I am distributing are the result of a fair amount of thought by me and they should be given equally serious thought by you. The division of assets outlined in the documents would have me to receive only approximately 40 percent of the company assets, which I would be willing to do if this or something similar is proposed by you. I believe something like this could be implemented by the end of the year to make the accounting work as simple as possible and operations could continue as normal until January 1, 2004. I don't believe anything would need changing with respect to Pine Ridge Enterprises, LLC [our hunting and guiding business].

If you would propose a dissolution of the company and division of the assets along the lines contained in the enclosed documents, I would probably agree to it. If you don't want to change the way the LLC is currently set up and the ranch assets are owned, then we will have a situation that I cannot believe you find tolerable. Under the current agreement I would continue to draw 50 percent of the profits or 100 percent of what your draws and benefits total. Under the current documents, I have a 50 percent vote and, because a majority is required for decisions, all decisions will have to be approved by me. I will no longer be willing to do the additional work and we will have to decide how to handle those expenses and see if we can reach a majority agreement on a plan for avoiding running completely out of money. I do not foresee that I will agree to permit your heirs to become substitute members after you pass away and I currently plan to allow them simply to be "assignees" that will have no voting rights in the company.

If you are agreeable to a dissolution of the company and a division of assets, I would have no objection if you want to allocate your life insurance policies to yourselves. I understand that there would be little tax consequence to dissolving the company and the transfer of the policies on your lives to yourselves or to a new company you might form would not change the tax-free nature of the insurance benefits.

The enclosed documents are fairly thorough in describing a way that the company could be divided and dissolved. There are other details that you may want to include in a proposal, but most of the questions regarding division of assets are addressed by what I have prepared. This type of division has the advantage of allowing you to retire as you see fit yet with more financial freedom and a lower work level and time commitment due to a decrease in farming activity requirements. It also would involve the potential for an increased net income because of a significant reduction in the expenses of farming. Please give this serious thought and then I believe we should meet or talk again to see if any agreements can be made."

Those words started my journey of making my own way. In the division spreadsheets, this initial approach concluded with the ranch retaining 60.79% of the total ranch value, while my side retained 39.21%. It is important to point out as well that based on our net income history, this split left the ranch with 67.5% of the income potential, while it left me with 32.5%. Most importantly, the numbers I used to develop an equitable division were based strictly upon written appraisals.

Unfortunately, my partners became extremely ill-mannered toward me after this discussion. Rather than getting together and talking about options and working together to determine what would be best for everyone involved, they refused to talk with me further and the situation began to escalate out of control.

About two months later my partners responded and I was disappointed, but not surprised, with their response. Instead of seeking legal counsel, they consulted a friend who was a financial planner and when I received his written correspondence, I remember laughing out loud when I read some of his claims. When I read the actual proposal, it was no laughing matter. This document was unfair and completely unreasonable in nearly every way. By staying at the ranch, and leaving things unchanged, I would eventually retain 100 percent of the management authority if I outlived the other partners. In addition, I would hold on to my current 50 percent ownership interest. If I left, as I had suggested to them in the first document, I would leave with 40 percent. I struggled with this because I knew it was completely unfair. Nonetheless, the glitch in the estate planned called for this change if the ranch was ever split or sold. In their proposal to me, they deflated that number even further, all the way down to 29 percent and that was insulting to me. That's why I wrote earlier that unreasonable and irrational people cannot be negotiated with. They do not see things as they are. They only see them as they want them to be.

In their proposal, the primary big differences involved land. When like-kind properties and locations of those properties were compared side to side, everything on my side of the ledger was listed at over twice the value of the property listed on their side of the ledger. Pretty tricky, right? That would give them twice the acres and left me with half as much, even though the end percentages matched up in their calculations. Other miscalculations were more obvious. All in all, they had deflated 51.8% of the items on their side of the ledger and inflated 24.5% of the items on my side. Seeing that the battle had now begun, I wrote the following letter to them in response:

"I have received a letter from your financial planner enclosed with a proposal written by both of you. I have briefly reviewed both the letter and the proposal. In a general sense, I wish to present to you some of my concerns regarding this information. First, the letter from your financial planner states that "...Joe and Jim brought to me a well-prepared proposal that [Ron] had prepared and presented to them as to how Rabou Ranch LLC might be dissolved and assets distributed." The documents I

presented to you both were merely ideas and suggestions on how, if at all, Rabou Ranch LLC may be split fairly and equitably between all partners. These materials were far from a proposal and nothing was offered to you through such documents. I documented our conversation from our initial meeting on October 22 and stressed multiple times to you both, despite what your personal interpretation may have been, that I was not proposing anything. I made it quite clear that I was only offering ideas on how things may work for all partners to continue operating in the capacity of production agriculturalists.

Secondly, the letter states that "Joe's and Jim's values are heavily influenced by their observations of production and carrying capacity of the various parcels of real estate as well as the location as it relates to ranch operations." Your observations are just that; they are observations. They are not backed with any factual information, nor are they consistent with what I have observed in your proposal.

As noted above, I have received your proposal regarding the division of the Rabou Ranch LLC assets. I find this proposal to be quite unacceptable. Since it is the first official proposal, determined as such by the title as well as the information your financial planner presented in his letter, I will be submitting a counter proposal to you after the first of the year. Generally speaking, your proposal raises multiple concerns. Some of these concerns include but are not limited to:

1) The land division is not an equitable division regarding value, location, terrain and aesthetic nature. At a quick glance it is obvious that this division is lopsided to benefit only the both of you. For such a division, your opinion on value is not comparable to that of a professional real estate appraiser.

2) The equipment division is not fashioned to suit the needs of both parties. This is again obvious since you both appear to wish to retain most of the newer equipment and/or more production efficient equipment.

3) A cattle, hay and wheat division needs to involve a precise, professional analysis of current market prices when and if an actual division were to occur.

4) A financial division will need to be based on current values to help balance the overall division. Reports involving the past 1 to 2 years withdrawals from financial institutions, funds and life insurance policies will also need to be conducted to determine if any funds were drawn by any partner for personal gain without equal treatment to existing partners. The numbers for liquid assets including the cash surrender value of life insurance policies will need to be determined at or close to the date of an overall division if one were to occur.

5) Pine Ridge Enterprises LLC is a separate entity and will not be included in a possible division of Rabou Ranch LLC.

6) The ideas I presented to you on October 22, 2003 involved a very fair and equitable approach that could have worked very well for all three partners and no harm was intended by presenting such ideas. Those initial ideas even suggested a larger percentage for the both of you. I have noted the manipulation of figures in your proposal so it seems that you both could realize even further gain. Nearly 52 percent of the figures on your side were deflated from my original figures, which were largely based on a 2003 documented appraisal of Rabou Ranch LLC. Only about 2 percent of the figures on your side were inflated, while nearly 25 percent of the figures on my side were inflated. Only approximately 10 percent of the figures on my side were deflated. While I can accept some deviation from a portion of numbers, these levels are clearly unacceptable.

As I have mentioned to you over the past several weeks, I would like to maintain a positive relationship with you both throughout this process. It is my hope that all partners can come to an agreement in a timely manner that is accurately defined and equitably representative. I will look forward to meeting with you both sometime in January."

136

Unfortunately, we never met again after our initial meeting. Even on the day of closing, my partners refused to attend and assigned their lawyer to do it for them.

After having processed their proposal, I spent the next few weeks writing my counterproposal in response; all 173 pages of it. I'll spare you the details in that document, but I mention the following in the introduction:

"The enclosed documents are a counterproposal to Joe's and Jim's proposal regarding the division of Rabou Ranch LLC. On October 22, Ron provided Joe and Jim with ideas on how a ranch division could be positive for all three partners and their families. The documents Ron presented at that time were suggestions that could perhaps serve as a guideline if Joe and Jim were so inclined to propose a split up. Joe's and Jim's proposal to Ron is unsatisfactory because it does not present an equitable and viable division. The following counterproposal provides a very equitable and reasonable way to divide the assets of Rabou Ranch LLC as well as explanations as to why it is equitable. Ron's original suggestions were offered as possibilities for fairness to all partners and, in fact, suggested that if those ideas were followed closely, Joe and Jim would end up with slightly more than 60 percent of the Rabou Ranch LLC assets. Ron's suggestions were presented as possibilities out of fairness to Joe and Jim and their families. As Ron mentioned in a meeting where all three were present on October 22, Ron didn't feel that it was fair for him to tell Joe and Jim what they could or couldn't do regarding their shares in Rabou Ranch LLC. Ron explained the following six points in a cover letter as well as in the partnership discussion on October 22, as to why he thought the current situation should be changed: 1) Ron indirectly owns a portion of Joe's and Jim's life insurance policies; 2) Ron will receive [dollar amount] from each of Joe's and Jim's life insurance policies upon their death if their family wish to become partners; 3) Joe's and Jim's family members that choose to become partners in Rabou Ranch LLC will be assignee

owners only and will have no voting rights or management control; 4) in theory, their assignee ownership will allow Ron to control 100 percent of the Rabou Ranch LLC management; 5) because of the way the current agreements are drawn, Ron will draw 50 percent of the profits from Rabou Ranch LLC or 100 percent of what Joe's and Jim's draws total, whichever is greater, whether Ron is physically working at Rabou Ranch LLC or not; and 6) all decisions will need to be approved by Ron because of his 50 percent membership rights.

In this counterproposal Ron has offered a fair and equitable division regarding monetary value, locations, income potential, and aesthetic and historic value. This counterproposal is divided into five sections: 1) land, buildings and improvements division; 2) machinery and equipment division; 3) liquid asset division involving cows, replacement heifers, bulls, calves, wheat, hay, straw, cash values of life insurance policies and bank accounts; 4) other remaining divisions; and 5) summary of results."

Upon receipt of this document, my partners finally chose to seek legal counsel. Their attorney attempted to send written letters I interpreted as threats to comply. I did not seek legal counsel in response. Rather, I formed my own response to these threats. I literally had nothing to lose and at that point I was not about to accept threats from an arrogant attorney. It only took about 3 months from this point until we settled. And where did we end up? Nearly exactly the same place I had originally suggested. From an ag production perspective, it truly was a reasonable and equitable way to divide assets. My biggest regret in the years that followed the division was that I did not advocate strongly enough for myself. I deceived myself into thinking that if I would just take less, we could keep our family relationships intact. I later realized the only way that was possible was if I had given it all to them and walked away with nothing.

In the end, for my partners, the entire cattle operation and our best farm ground remained whole and they were able to function the way things had always been. They only lacked a few outlying properties, some farm ground and two neglected and dilapidated building sites, which were all included on my side of the division. Nearly all our equipment was extremely outdated, but I even compromised and allowed them to have the better equipment. I began my operation with three small tractors ranging in horsepower from 50 to 130 and ranging in age from over 20 years to 50 years old. I had a few older implements, a couple old dump trucks, and some miscellaneous pieces. After I began to build my farm, the first used tractor I purchased cost more than twice as much as the value of all the equipment combined from the ranch split. We began with about 800 acres of deeded farmland, some deeded outlying pastures and no cows.

I was 30 years old when I first approached my partners with ideas on how to divide things amongst ourselves. There are many lessons I have learned along the way, some of which I have already shared in this book. As you think about your own family and your own situation, let me share a few more that I hope you will find helpful.

PROPER COUNSEL

First, never underestimate the value of proper counsel. And I don't mean just legal and financial counsel. I mean counsel from mentors; individuals who can offer support and honest advice throughout the process. My mentors were older men who were well versed in dealing with family issues. Some had been in the ranching business, while others had not. Their wisdom helped guide me in some of the darkest times in my life. As an outsider looking in on the situation, they provided me with invaluable counsel and wisdom that I could not have found anywhere else. They provided a perspective that I could not see. When you are in the battle, it's difficult to see and understand the war. These mentors were men I could trust with my life and still do today. I'm not the smartest person out there, but my goal has always been to surround myself with people who are. My father always told me you become who you associate with. That could not be more true.

Proper counsel also comes in the form of talking with your spouse and understanding his or her perspective as well. In our family ranch, ironically enough, the women never had much of a say in anything regarding the ranching operation, even though my great-great grandmother was the one who originally homesteaded it well over one hundred years ago. As a result, for me, that has been a hurdle I have had to learn to clear. I had to develop an understanding that even though my wife didn't come from an agriculture background, she still has valuable insight as to how we need to move forward in our business and with our family. I've learned that her perception is often much more accurate than my own and that I just need to trust her natural intuition. Work together with your spouse to determine the best long-term solution for both of you and your family will benefit as a result.

Finally, proper counsel most especially comes in the form of a professional who can help you through the process from start to finish. In most cases, hiring an ag consultant may be the best money you'll ever spend. Doing so helps to create a level and unbiased playing field for all parties involved. A consultant can help create a framework that will protect the families, business, employee and generational changes by establishing a very clear alignment of expectations. Many farms and ranches, though they may be formed as LLCs, S-Corps or C-Corps with corresponding operating agreements, do not have a specific corporate structure. An organizational chart, marking the flow of multiple entities, decision making and job responsibilities, written job descriptions, employment policies and requirements, written vision and mission statements, safety policies, standard operating procedures (SOPs), leadership roles, financial policies, budget development and implementation and financial reporting, trend sheets and corporate culture are all critical parts of any successful business. A consultant's overarching goal is to help create a system and process that will allow the family and business to consistently and effectively solve problems as they arise in the future. This structure provides direction and operational stability for the company even if family members no longer serve in active leadership roles. The American Society of Agricultural Consultants is a great resource that can lead you to a consultant who will best meet your needs. For more information visit www.agconsultants.org.

Every industry in the world follows a well-defined structure, yet family farms and ranches do not hold themselves to the same standard. The problem is most farms and ranches do not view this approach as a necessary part of doing business. I would argue the contrary; I believe it is absolutely imperative. And more so today than it has ever been. Had our family had an appropriate structure that was clearly stated and understood, a great deal of the issues we faced would have been immediately solved, thus preventing the continuation of the build-up of strife and resentment that eventually contributed to our demise. When policies can be created in a business and used as the basis for decision making, the emotional component is diminished and personal bias and influence can be properly controlled. I can attest that death changes how people interact with each other and it changes their perception of how things should be. Proper and well-defined structure takes the guesswork out of "what happens if…". Not deciding to change is still deciding. The results will just not be what you hoped for.

THINK

Second, don't just react. Think. Look introspectively. And take your time. Good things do not happen overnight and complex businesses and family matters take a lot of thought and deliberation. Look at all sides of the situation and try to see the others' perspective. As we struggled in the years after my father's death, my wife and I concluded the problem may very well be us, so we sought out to change ourselves and our reaction to our circumstances. We allowed ourselves to be humbled by not reacting, but truly listening to the other side and reported back to our mentors for their evaluation and advice. And while the conclusions proved that it takes two to have an argument, the disagreements we continued to have didn't have any reasonable solutions. Unless we were to completely submit to the other side and their approach to running the business and how they lived their lives, it was very clear things would have to change.

There were days when I would work at the ranch and think to myself how great it was and how I would hate to ever have it be any different. Then there were days where I knew, without a doubt, that things must change. Those feelings haunted me each day. I was hot and cold and it seemed to just depend on the day. I became tired of my own indecisiveness. I decided I would have to take out the emotion and look at the situation as objectively as possible. The question I asked myself was this: Even if I liked every moment all the time, what would happen if something happened to me like it did to my father? Would the resulting position be healthy for my wife or my children? Would it be fair to them? The answer was a resounding no. Because of that I decided to change.

It's hard to make good decisions if you are constantly operating with your feelings. It's like being married. You may not always feel the bliss of marriage like you once did, but you don't kick your spouse out of the house because of it. You consciously decide to love and honor that commitment no matter what you may feel from day to day.

ACT WITH FAIRNESS
& INTEGRITY

Third, play fair and act with integrity. Don't be the person to cheat, even if it means you end up with less. You still have to sleep with yourself at night. My parent's home was on the main ranch compound and as part of our agreement, the partner's son-in-law who worked for us was to move out of the home on one of the places I received then move into my parent's home. Without a doubt, everyone knew the work my parents put into their home and it showed. It was the nicest house on the ranch. I knew the house I was to receive in exchange was not even close to the same quality and I assumed that the son-in-law and his family that were living in there had probably not done the greatest job in caring for it. Nonetheless, the homes were to be exchanged in "good, clean condition". After the exchange, what I was not prepared for was the utter disrespect, destruction and filthiness I found in the other house. While my mother cleaned her own home and made sure her home presented well, my relatives had no intention of doing the same thing. When I entered the home, the smell of urine was incomprehensible. Either they or their animals had urinated in every room, on the walls and on the floors. They had let the mice completely overtake the house and there were thousands upon thousands of mouse droppings throughout the house. The mice had eaten through shelving, walls and flooring, and they had made sure that in the move, they took nearly every light fixture, every socket and every switch. No cleaning company would touch the house and I had to hire a home restoration expert to sanitize the entire home at the cost of nearly $9000. Whenever I tell people of this story, they find it hard to believe, but when I show them the pictures, the evidence is overwhelming.

I worked with my attorney to file a lawsuit against my relatives for breach of the contract and for raising their children in such an environment. My attorney said there was no doubt I would win. At the last moment I decided to drop the suit, fix things up myself and move on. It was just one more way for them to display their lack of integrity. In my mind, suing them and winning would not change them or the circumstances.

When you live in small-town America, one thing you come to realize very quickly is how untouchable some of the "big fish" perceive themselves to be. I honestly think my relatives thought there was nothing they couldn't do or say that others wouldn't go along with. When I "broke the mold" I think they were appalled that their own perceived authoritativeness held no ground with me. Just because you have more money, a bigger farm or have lived in an area the longest, you are not given a free pass to take advantage of others. Yet there are people all across our great country that act in this regard. It is disgusting, it is shameful and it is downright wrong.

Recently I was involved in a land deal that seemed it would be a good fit for us. The land was listed through a real estate agent and when my realtor discovered it was going to come on the market, we asked to write the first offer. When I looked at the price and ran the numbers for return on investment, I decided to proceed with a full price offer. The seller accepted the offer and we were set to close a couple months out. During the negotiation process I received a copy of the current arrangement between the owner and the farmer who was renting the ground. I was informed that the farmer had tried to purchase the land from the owner at less than half the price. When the owner disagreed, they listed the property on the open market. When I received a copy of their lease agreement, to my surprise the farmer had a provision in his lease for a 60 day first right of refusal "in the event that the Lessor shall at any time during or after the lease term desire to sell the demised premises pursuant to any bona fide offer which it shall have received in writing, it shall offer them to Lessee at the same price as that contained in such bona fide offer". What was surprising to me was that when a landowner signed this lease, he or she would be indefinitely locked into a legal obligation to offer the property to this farmer even if the lease had long since expired. Though some may look at this provision as just a part of doing business, I have never seen this provision in a farming lease and would never personally lock anyone I farm for into such a contract.

Recently, I heard of another farmer in our area who is doing the same thing with his older landowners. Unbeknownst to them, he is inserting this clause in their new agreements once the old ones have expired and not informing them of the change. The way I see it, if I do a good job farming for the landowner and act with integrity in doing so, it is highly likely they will consider me first if they ever decide to sell the property. If you are out to control everyone you do business with, then I suppose this provision is a necessity. Other provisions in this lease, such as locking the land up for 10 years with an automatic renewal and saddling the landowner with 100 percent of the cost of government program requirements are very lopsided to benefit only the Lessee. In addition, in no portion of the lease were there any provisions about properly caring for the land. As a landowner, it is critical to understand what you are committing to and even more important to understand who you are dealing with.

In the end, the farmer exercised his first right of refusal and we did not end up with the purchase. I personally have no problem with that. But here's where I do have a problem; I am the one to blame. It sounds completely foolish. The farmer has taken the stance to inform people in our community that I "cost him a couple hundred thousand dollars". The problem with the big fish in the small pond ego is that the big fish think they are justified in rolling over everyone in pursuit of building their empire. When the big fish are challenged, they cannot accept the fact that other fish live in the same pond as well.

Here's where the confusion begins; a first right of refusal does not exempt the seller from asking for whatever price they want and does not grant the holder the authority to demand whatever price they determine. A first right of refusal just allows the holder the opportunity to match any price another party is willing to pay. That is how the free market works. The real issue is not that I am to blame, the real issue is the big fish doesn't think anyone else should be capable of participating in the free market. If any buyer is willing to pay fair market value, the big fish becomes upset he can't steal the property for less than half price. I love it when the free market works. And if that means I am unable to purchase a property for fair market value because there is an existing holder of a first right of refusal and that right is exercised, I am truly happy with the outcome. The moral of the story is this; uphold your end of the bargain, even if you don't get what you want. There will be other opportunities. Don't tie the hands of the people you are doing business with. Any agreement that is good and worthwhile will always be beneficial for both parties.

Remember you are always setting an example. What example do you want that to be? Your children and grandchildren will know the truth someday so what side will you choose to be on? I firmly believe in the law of compensation. In other words, what goes around comes around. Dishonesty and deceit, while it may seem like a good idea at the time, will always come with a price. What

I mean by playing fair is to not roll over and wet yourself. You are absolutely entitled to stand strong and to be tough in negotiations.

What I mean is you can still act with decency and integrity. If you cannot uphold your own character, what do you have? In the end it may be all you're left with. In the freest country the world has ever known, that is all you need. You can rebuild. We did. You can reinvent yourself. We did. You can start over. We did. You can make it better than it has ever been. We did. In the end, don't cheat yourself, but also don't cheat others.

BE FLEXIBLE

Fourth, be flexible. If you find you aren't getting exactly what you want in the negotiation process, think outside the box. Take a long hard look at the assets on your side of the ledger and think about all their potential possibilities. Think big and think outside of the industry you are in. For example, as I evaluated the pieces of land I received in the split, I identified other potential uses for those parcels besides just their agricultural value.

When you are looking at your own operation, pay particular attention to properties that have public road access, water and recreation and hunting potential. Stay away from large blocks of land that cannot be easily divided, land that has only a singular use (for example only livestock grazing) and land that is landlocked by property owned by others. Stay away from properties that contain dump sites and multiple houses. Dump sites are a major issue in today's world and can severely diminish the value of your property. I wasn't interested in the ranch headquarters because there were too many houses, corrals and old barns that were largely singular in their potential use. Additionally, multiple large dump sites were on the property and the land base those headquarters provided for was much too small. Even had the ranch stayed fully intact, the land base was realistically too small to justify that many houses and outbuildings.

During our split, I was interested in stand-alone properties, such as where our farm headquarters are. These are properties that will retain a higher value because they are more marketable to a larger audience. Over time, we have improved our property to function as a farm on one side and then as a residence and personal retreat with commercial potential on the other. It has a highly functional and diverse use for us, but also would provide that to nearly any other buyer, whether they were involved in agriculture or not. And it's not so much that it creates a burdensome tax bill. It can be kept up to date without a lot of extra expense and effort because of the initial investment we poured into it. I'll touch on that a bit in the next few paragraphs.

When I made the decision to finally look at my operation as a business rather than an heirloom, I took a very close look at all my assets and their return. I decided that if I was going to stay in business in production agriculture and develop positive cash flow in my operation, I would have to make some very hard choices. On the property where my relatives severely damaged the home, we fixed the house and outbuildings, surveyed off 35 acres and sold it for over 4 times what we had into it. The property wasn't serving any purpose for us and those proceeds helped open opportunities for other properties that had a much higher return. We did that with numerous other properties as well, both on and off the farm. The key is to get creative and see potential in circumstances above and beyond what others can see. To be perfectly honest, there were some decisions we made with land sales that were extremely difficult for me. They were very emotionally taxing. But in the end, they have been extremely good decisions for our operation and our future. For some of you reading this, this approach may seem completely absurd to you. I understand that. But have enough vision to look beyond yourself and where you are today and what you are currently doing. You cannot predict the future and unforeseen circumstances can change your life completely.

I always assess each situation and deal from a worst-case scenario perspective. In other words, if everything went to heck and I had to change what I was doing, would I be trapped or would I have options? Give yourself options. You may never have to exercise those options, but if the need or desire ever arises, you'll be glad you gave yourself that flexibility. As we have sold assets and reinvested in assets, we have increased our net worth substantially. In land and buildings only, our original split was 40 percent on my side and 60 percent on the ranch side. Because of the changes we have made over the past 15 years, from a market value position in relation to agriculture production, those numbers have changed to be over 70% my side and 30% on the ranch side when combining the values of both operations. Regarding combined cattle and equipment, those numbers have changed from 40%/60% to about 80% my side, 20% ranch side. In addition, our business generates over 5 times more annual revenue than our entire ranching operation did when it was fully intact. It's important to know your business and pay attention to numbers. A little bit of creative maneuvering and willingness to change can have a drastic impact on your cash flow and balance sheet.

LONG TERM VIABILITY

Fifth, look at long term viability. I have already described some ways in which you can give yourself some flexibility and options, but I want to break that down even further. One thing I think most of us rely on in production agriculture is the fact that we will always be there to keep the operation moving forward. In too many instances, this is not the case. A sudden death, freak accident, sudden change in health or maybe even just a shift in desires can change everything. Don't put yourself in a box where you have little or no options.

One thing I have always kept in mind when building my operation is its potential for passive income. Passive income is income that can be earned with little or no effort on your part. If you were to walk away today either voluntarily or because of extenuating circumstances, what is the potential of your assets to create income for you and your family? I like giving myself lots of options because the future is unknown. Because my father's shares of the ranch were locked up in the corporation and because he was only a 25 percent owner, the opportunity to produce income from his shares provided absolutely nothing to my mother. What she was left with were the proceeds from a small life insurance policy and any money she and my father were able to save over the life of their marriage, which as you might imagine, living on $600 a month, wasn't much. When she moved off the ranch after we split the operation, my partners refused to give her anything for her home, even though it was she and my father who put their personal money into it. As a result, most everything she had went into a place for her to live off the ranch.

Ask yourself this question, "If I were to walk away from my entire operation today, what benefit would it provide for me, my wife or the rest of my family?" It's true that our farms and our ranches are our homes and our lifestyle, but we must look beyond that. They are an investment and must be treated as such. There are many properties and farmsteads in our area where people live and haven't taken care of them or where owners have moved away and let them just fall apart. Then, the new owners have never taken the initiative to improve those sites or even clean them up. I drive by a farmstead every day that one of my neighbors has let completely fall apart. The barn has fallen in, the house is in shambles and the trees and yard are completely unkempt. The place is too far gone now, but had he initially just invested some time, effort and a little bit of money fixing things up, he could have used the property as either a rental that would have produced passive income or he could have surveyed off a few acres and sold it for a significant profit.

One of the things I like so much about land is that it is a tangible asset. It's something you can put your hands on and fully control its use over both the short and long term. And it is an investment that can be leveraged to purchase additional assets. Farmland has been a great investment for us. I know what my return is on the farmland I own when I produce crops from it myself and I know what that return is if I were to have someone else farm it for me. That provides a significant benefit to me because it provides me with options. And if something were to happen to me, it gives my wife and my children options as well. Our current operation has more passive income earning opportunity than our entire ranch did when it was fully intact. And not only is it more, but it doesn't need to be split between 3 or 4 different families. It is ours in its entirety.

As I mentioned earlier, the investment into buildings and multiple houses on one "compound" is not a good investment. Many farms and ranches in our area contain so many houses and buildings, it becomes a burden in both time and money to properly care for them. Many of these facilities have been pieced together over time rather than being built soundly both architecturally and functionally the first time. I have seen places where buildings have collapsed and the owners haven't even taken the time to clean them up. I have seen places where the owners use different colors of siding and other materials on the same building or home probably because it was cheap. I have also seen places that once had great homes and outbuildings, but as time has passed, those have been abandoned and left to rot, rather than being cared for. Everything you do on your place matters. That goes all the way from proper building maintenance, building functionality, grounds and landscaping, control of noxious weeds and cleaning up old equipment and junk piles.

When we landed on my grandparent's place after the ranch split, we were left with buildings that were rotting and filthy, a house that was in dire need of attention inside and out and even an outdated water system and collapsed septic system. My grandparents did the best they could, but as they aged, it was clear there was a lot that had been neglected. Nearly all the money the ranch ever made went into the main ranch compound and my grandparent's place never received the attention it needed. My wife and I initially moved into my grandparent's home for just the summer months when we were building the farm. I remember she used to sit in the living room with our first son when he was a baby because I had installed a small air conditioning unit and it was the only place in the house it was tolerable to live. I remember sitting in the living room in the evenings watching the mice run back and forth across the room and under our furniture. I remember opening the top door to our cistern that held the drinking water for the house so I could fish out the dead mice floating in the water. And I remember the big hole near the house that I nearly fell in one night when navigating myself through the yard. As it turned out, the septic tank had collapsed and when we dug it up, the only thing that was left was the bottom of the metal tank.

As we have grown our operation over time, nearly everything we have ever made has gone directly back into improving our headquarters and into growing our operation. I never saw any use in keeping old buildings around if they didn't suit a specific purpose for our family or our operation. We began by cleaning out the existing buildings. It was an enormous task because I think my family had saved just about everything since the beginning of time. I began by taking the stance that if I didn't know what it was (much of what I found was for equipment we owned once upon a time), or if it was broken, I threw it away or recycled it. I remember cleaning out bolt bins that were full of over 500 pounds of broken and stripped bolts. I guess they were being saved to one day rethread. As far as I was concerned, how much did a handful of new bolts really cost? A few bucks?

Some of you will disagree with me, I know. Your argument is that every dollar adds up. I would not disagree. However, if we can't rid our mind of the small things that are occupying it, we can never fully focus on a bigger picture; most especially one that can make a significant impact on our operation. Meanwhile, we are spending our time straightening staples in a vise and rethreading bolts and we fail to miss rehabbing a farm site that could mean tens of thousands in profit. I once heard a story from a John Deere man who said my relatives at the ranch were hounding him to pick up a rubber washer they had purchased as an extra and now they wanted their money back. They expected him to drive 100 miles round trip so they could get back their $1.58. Why not just keep it for when the one you just put in fails and you can move on with things? Don't spend so much time micromanaging pennies and then step over all the dollars in the process.

160

Most all the original buildings on our place no longer served a purpose, so we tore down some and re-purposed the rest. Those buildings were all given new matching metal roofs, new steel siding, insulation, new electric and new windows. We converted an old dirt floor barn to a guest lounge and music studio, complete with sound equipment, full bar, pool and foosball tables, knotty pine and laminate wood flooring. An old leaning garage was reframed after it was straightened and was turned into a large commercial kitchen facility with running water, stainless steel work areas, walk-in cooler, heat and air conditioning, big screen TV and Wifi, in addition to a large office area on the other side. An old wood granary with rotten walls no longer attached to the footers, sunken walls from side to side and large holes in the roof was converted to a 9 bed, 2 bath guest lodge with living room, Wifi, satellite TV, heat and air conditioning, full with other modern conveniences and amenities guests might expect.

These buildings now not only serve a purpose for our family and our guests, but also serve the hunters we host throughout the year with our company Black Canyon Outfitters, Inc. They allow us to host on farm experiences, corporate retreats and on farm tours for our grain buyers. We were able to keep my grandparent's original home and there is nothing in the house we haven't fully redone. Not only did we make the house nicer, safer and more energy efficient than it has ever been, we also added onto it, tripling the square footage. We also changed the exterior in its entirety and chose colors and architecture that allow the home to stand out as a centerpiece of the property yet compliment the rest of the surrounding structures.

The right kind of land serves as a tremendous opportunity to create passive income, but so do the right facilities if they are built correctly. Those facilities can also serve as another source of passive income, as well as helping to develop diversity in your operation. Be aware of the opportunities that your property can create while you are operating and be mindful of what they can continue to create if you are not.

This place, originally purchased by Margaret Rabou, served as home to Frank & Dorothy Rabou for 62 years and is now the headquarters for Rabou Farms, Inc. and home of Ron & Julie Rabou

INVOLVE THE NEXT GENERATION - NOW

Last, involve the next generation now. If your operation currently involves or will involve the next generation, as hard as it may be, release some control and allow that generation to begin to have a say in what happens now and over the long haul. I can't tell you how many times when I was growing up that I heard from my dad's cousins at the ranch, "Us guys know what's best. You kids need to just do what you're told." Or "It's nothing you need to concern yourself with." And my least favorite of all, "That's a good boy." Wow! Last I checked I wasn't your dog. I demand some respect too.

We are now surrounded by a generation of young people who will never not have an answer to a question. Trillions of bits of information are at our fingertips. And even though information is readily and easily accessible, there are just plain too many things in business that can't be learned or understood without experience. Experience is best gained when it is accompanied by solid mentorship, coupled with an understanding for self-discipline and constructive criticism.

It is hard to accept responsibility when no responsibility is ever given. On one hand, if we expect nothing of others, that's exactly what we'll get. On the other, if we expect great things, we'll be shocked at how our expectations will be exceeded. I've seen too many operations where the father is in his eighties and the son or daughter is in his or her sixties and they are still treated like a hired hand. They've never been allowed to make decisions and one day when they'll have to, their ability to think clearly and make the right decisions for the right reasons will be paralyzed.

Allow the younger generation to make some mistakes. Invaluable lessons will be learned and remembered and in

163

doing so, maybe everyone will discover new and better ideas along the way. Help to create and facilitate an environment that encourages input and ideas and fosters a sense of belonging and trust.

CONCLUSION

As I bring things to a close, remember that it's never too early to begin planning for the future. If you are in a situation like I was, it's likely things will never change for the better unless you act. You don't have to step out immediately and cause a massive amount of turbulence in your operation, but what you can do is begin to thoroughly think through your options and take baby steps in working toward where you want to be.

For the most part, no one likes change. It's hard, it's uncomfortable and it takes effort. And although change can be pretty rough at times, without it, things are bound to get rougher. Remember that doing nothing is still doing something and failing to make a decision is still making a decision. There is no stagnation. We are all in a constant state of change. The question we must ask ourselves is "do we want to move forward or do we want to fall further backward?" Our operation at the ranch hadn't changed in so long and so many problems had never been addressed, we were finally at a point where things had to change drastically.

Remember that no matter how much control we think we have, we are not the ultimate authority. No one can predict the future, but you can begin to shape your own future by planning with an open mind, being honest with yourself and allowing yourself to build and retain an arsenal of options. You can honor your heritage and still live life on your own terms. Don't measure your success by thinking your farm or ranch must continue like it always has. Take control of your own business and you will create your own heritage. Don't tie all your identity up with what you do or where you come from, no matter how much you value your family's history. Strive to keep a work/life balance and remember your legacy isn't just what you do and what you own; it's most especially who you are, the example you set for others and by your actions, who you can teach them to be. Your legacy is about making things better. Only YOU can make your OWN way. Today is a great day to begin.

ABOUT THE AUTHOR

Ron Rabou is the CEO of Rabou Farms, Inc., President of the Rabou Companies and a principle with Agrite Solutions, LLC. Ron is a true entrepreneur with a career thus far that includes a combination of over 25 years of public speaking, communications training, public relations, fundraising, foundation and private business experience. Ron is co-author of a self-help book, "Keep it Simple: The 12 Core Values that Lead to Personal and Professional Success" and past host of "ReThink on the Radio". In 2019 his farm was recognized by National Farm Journal Media as one of three national finalists for Top Producer of the Year. He is a member of the Cheyenne Rotary Club and a graduate of the University of Wyoming and resides on his farm near Albin, Wyoming with his wife and 3 sons.

Ron provides private business consulting for family farms and ranches and also speaks to audiences across the nation about the value of agriculture, organic agriculture production and family farm transition. For consulting services or to book Ron for your event contact him at raboufarms@gmail.com

To learn more about Rabou Farms please visit **www.raboufarms.com**

To learn more about speaking and seminar topics please visit **www.ronrabou.com**

www.ingramcontent.com/pod-product-compliance
Lightning Source LLC
Chambersburg PA
CBHW040856210326
41597CB00029B/4863